The Origins and Evolution of Christmas

From Pagan Traditions to Modern Celebrations

By
Robert Enochs

Forward

The celebration of Christmas, with its twinkling lights, decorated trees, and familiar melodies, holds a special place in the hearts of millions around the world. But beneath the layers of modern festivities lies a tapestry of traditions, beliefs, and customs that span centuries and many cultures.

The origins of this holiday reveal an evolution as complex as it is fascinating, rooted in the ancient rhythms of seasonal change and in early religious practices that predate Christianity by thousands of years.

This book invites readers to explore not only the holiday's historical context but also its ongoing transformation in our modern, interconnected world. We delve into how Christmas became a symbol of warmth, family, and goodwill, reflecting the shared human desire for hope and connection during winter's coldest days.

Alongside this, we examine the influence of commercialism, cultural adaptation, and globalized media in shaping the celebration as we know it.

The story of Christmas is layered, diverse, and filled with centuries-old mysteries that make this beloved holiday as fascinating as it is festive.

The Origins and Evolution of Christmas: From Pagan Traditions to Modern Celebrations takes you on a journey through the transformations of this holiday, from ancient rituals and pagan roots to the celebration we know today.

This book is the second installment in the *Mysteries of Tradition* series, following *The Origins and Evolution of Halloween.* If you enjoy discovering the rich, often hidden histories behind our most cherished holidays, I encourage you to explore the Halloween volume, where you'll uncover similar insights and surprising connections between past and present.

If you find *The Origins and Evolution of Christmas* insightful or thought-provoking, please consider leaving a positive review on Amazon. Your feedback not only helps other readers find the book, but also signals to Amazon that this is a book worth sharing.

Thank you for joining this exploration of tradition, celebration, and cultural evolution.

Robert Enochs

Contents

Introduction

Christmas, with its twinkling lights and jingling bells, stands as one of the most cherished holidays around the globe. Yet, beneath the layers of merriment and festivity, lies a rich tapestry of history and culture woven through centuries.

This book dives into the fascinating evolution of Christmas, revealing how ancient rituals and beliefs intertwined with Christian traditions to form the celebration we know today. Understanding the origins of Christmas provides insight into a time when humanity sought to make sense of the world through the rhythm of nature, weaving festivals and rituals that echoed their hopes and fears.

The exchange of gifts, the warmth of a hearth, and the goodwill towards men—these emblematic traditions of Christmas are not mere modern embellishments. They trace back to various cultures and epochs that heralded the onset of winter.

Long before Christmas was ever celebrated as the birth of Christ, people around the world marked the winter solstice, a time when the sun seemed to pause in the sky, indicating the turning point of the year. These solstice celebrations, steeped in ancient rituals, provided the foundational blocks upon which later Christmas traditions were built.

This book unpacks the layers of *syncretism* (the practice of combining different beliefs and various schools of thought), and how Roman festivals like Saturnalia with its feasting and merrymaking became intertwined with the story of Christ's birth.

The transition from pagan traditions to Christian rites was not abrupt but a slow intertwining of cultures, rituals, and politics. The journey of Saint Nicholas from a beloved saint to the plump and jolly Santa Claus highlights how myths evolve and adapt through generations, reflecting the values and aspirations of the times.

The commercialization of Christmas, a more recent phenomenon, adds another layer to the intricate history of the holiday. While the spiritual and communal aspects of Christmas are celebrated, the holiday has also become a significant economic driver.

It influences global markets and reflects cultural shifts, illuminated by the ever-present glow of screens and advertisements. This interplay of commerce and tradition forms part of the current Christmas narrative, revealing how societal changes continue to shape our holiday experiences.

Modern Christmas traditions are a blend of ancient and new, sacred and secular, local and global. The way we celebrate Christmas today has been significantly influenced by literature and media.

Iconic tales and films have worked their way into the core of Christmas traditions, further entailing the holiday's role as a time for storytelling and reflection. With the rise of technology and awareness of environmental concerns, contemporary Christmas celebrations continue to evolve, capturing the spirit of the age while paying homage to the past.

In exploring the ever-evolving cultural and historical significance of Christmas, this book aims to illuminate the diverse influences that have shaped the holiday over centuries. By delving into the origins and transformations of Christmas, readers can better appreciate the complexity and depth of this beloved celebration.

Importance of Understanding Pre-Christian Traditions

Grasping the essence of pre-Christian traditions is like unearthing the roots of a tree, helping us see where Christmas draws some of its life-giving nutrients.

These ancient customs and beliefs provide clues about why certain Christmas symbols and rituals exist today. When we understand these origins, we're not just looking back; we're gaining a fuller picture of how this beloved holiday took shape, blending layers of meaning over centuries.

Before Christianity spread across Europe and beyond, winter solstice marked a time of celebration and reflection for many cultures. It wasn't only about the shortest day of the year.

Instead, it was steeped in themes of renewal and survival, ideas that would later be woven into the fabric of Christmas. In appreciating these earlier traditions, we can start to comprehend why people in the past found solace and hope as the days began to lengthen once more.

Moreover, acknowledging these pre-Christian traditions shows a narrative of adaptability and continuity. It highlights humans' enduring ability to reshape their spiritual expressions while holding onto threads of the past.

By incorporating these earlier elements with newer ones, early Christian missionaries were able to make their faith more relatable and acceptable to those they sought to convert. Recognizing this syncretism is essential, as it tells a fuller, richer story of religious and cultural evolution.

Understanding pre-Christian practices also encourages us to see the ingenuity and resourcefulness in early cultural exchanges. This perspective invites a dialogue about how ideas adapt and persist, acting as cultural bridges rather than barriers.

It enriches our appreciation of Christmas by shedding light on its diverse and shared human heritage, reminding us that holidays are living traditions, continuously influenced by the spirits and beliefs that preceded them.

Chapter 1:
Historical Context of Winter
Solstice Celebrations

The winter solstice has long held profound significance across many early cultures, embodying the year's darkest night and the pivotal point where light begins its return.

It's a time that has intrigued and inspired humankind for millennia, marking not only a celestial event but also a deeply spiritual one. Ancient societies, from the Norse in Scandinavia to the Germanic tribes and Celts, recognized this transformative period with various ceremonies and rituals. Their festivities were often imbued with the symbolism of darkness giving way to light, a natural metaphor for hope and renewal.

Looking back, the winter solstice wasn't just about celebrating the position and movement of the sun; it was a metaphysical marker for the death and rebirth of the sun itself.

In many cultures, this theme was essential. The sun, seen as a life-giving force, its 'death' at the solstice was a reminder of the ephemeral nature of life. Yet, its 'rebirth' signaled the promise of longer days ahead.

This recurring sequence mirrored the cycles found in nature—death, decay, and renewal—integral to agrarian societies that depended on the seasonal rhythms.

Moreover, the solstice often spanned a ceremonial period of three days, believed by some cultures to be the sun's transitional phase. Think of it as a cosmic pause, a sacred interval when the path of the sun seemed halted before shifting to ascendancy once more.

This time was ripe for myths and legends to take root, as people sought to interpret and explain these celestial activities. Rituals and myths developed around this mysterious interval created a tapestry of narratives that underscored the solstice's importance, not just as a climatic event but as a spiritual touchstone.

Winter Solstice in Early Cultures

The winter solstice, marking the year's shortest day and longest night, fascinated ancient civilizations.

They saw this as more than a celestial event; it was a profound turning point—a harbinger of renewal when hope sneaked back into daily life, promising the return of light and warmth. Numerous early cultures held diverse yet intriguingly similar celebrations during this pivotal time.

For many ancient peoples, the solstice was pivotal in their calendars, representing a critical moment of change in the natural world.

In Northern Europe, for instance, long before the familiar image of snow-covered chalets and twinkling lights emerged, peoples observed Yule. Honoring the Norse gods, this festival centered around fires, storytelling, and feasting. Families gathered in great halls, casting wishes into glowing Yule logs with the belief that such flames had the power to entice the sun to come back.

Elsewhere, ancient Egyptians celebrated their sky god Horus, and the Romans honored Saturn in their riotous festivities called Saturnalia. Both were imbued with a shared narrative of rebirth and a cycle that promised continuity with the cosmos.

These celebrations weren't just jubilant cries for a better tomorrow; they were intricate dances with time, mythology, and the universe, signifying a bond between humanity and the divine.

In the depths of Central America, the Maya incorporated solstice rituals into their rich tapestry of ceremony, aligning their awe-inspiring architecture with celestial events.

As day broke during the solstice, sunlight would grace the precise corners of their pyramids—an ethereal spectacle that seemed orchestrated by gods rather than men, a testament to their advanced understanding of the heavens.

These gatherings, although separated by thousands of miles, language barriers, and culture, shared a universal thread of symbolism and ritual.

The winter solstice's reverence was a common human thread, a serene acknowledgment that even in darkest times, brighter days would return. Understanding these early solstice celebrations underscores the gradually intertwining narratives that later shaped the holiday we now call Christmas.

Key Themes of the Winter Solstice

Throughout history, the winter solstice has captivated cultures, standing as a profound symbol of transformation and hope.

As the longest night of the year relinquishes its hold, ancient communities have seen it as a turning point, a moment when darkness begins to yield to the light.

This celestial event, marking the climax of the sun's inexorable journey from ascendancy to hibernation, invites reflection on themes transcending time and space. Central to these musings are the ideas of death and rebirth, encapsulating the intricacies of nature's cycles and the enduring human spirit.

The notion of the "Death and Rebirth of the Sun" is a cornerstone of solstice traditions. Many early cultures believed the sun, much like a deity, needed to be reborn each year to usher in spring's promise.

During the winter solstice, the sun's apparent pause in its southern descent, followed by its gradual return, symbolized this cyclical resurrection. Communities across the globe saw this period as one of regeneration, a time to cast away the dwindling light of the past and anticipate the rejuvenation brought by the new sun.

Closely linked to this concept is the "Three-Day Sequence of the Sun's Death and Rebirth". People observed that for three days, the sun appeared to stand still in the sky, an interval interpreted as a liminal* space between the end of the old solar year and the genesis of the new. This pause was a powerful spiritual metaphor for reflection, rest, and renewal, mirroring the cycles found in agriculture and human life.

These key themes have reverberated through time, influencing practices and beliefs far beyond their pagan origins.

As we're about to explore further in the book, such themes not only permeated pagan celebrations but also laid the groundwork for new traditions, including the development of Christmas itself.

This interplay of darkness and light, death and renewal, transcends the mere physical phenomena, inviting us into a deeper understanding of life's perennial potential for renewal and hope.

FootNotes:

"Liminal" refers to something related to a transitional or in-between state, phase, or condition. It often describes the threshold or boundary between two different stages, spaces, or experiences. The term comes from the Latin word *limen*, meaning "threshold."

Death and Rebirth of the Sun

The notion of the sun's death and rebirth is a fascinating aspect of winter solstice celebrations and serves as a poignant reminder of the cyclical nature of life.

During the colder months, ancient cultures noticed the days growing shorter and the nights longer, signaling the sun's apparent decline. However, the winter solstice marked the turning point, the promise of renewal as the sun reemerged, gradually reclaiming its strength.

This imagery of death and rebirth was powerful and pervasive across various early societies. For the Norse, it was Yule, a time to celebrate the sun's return with feasting and fire.

The ancient Romans observed Saturnalia, in part to honor the sun god and herald the gradual return of light. Similarly, the Egyptians celebrated the rebirth of Horus, which symbolized the triumph of light over darkness.

These themes weren't just about celestial phenomena but were deeply embedded in the hopeful rhythms of agriculture. The return of the sun hinted at warmer weather and fertile lands.

It was a signal that life, both plant and animal, would soon flourish once more. The interplay between darkness and light, death and life, became not just a seasonal event but a spiritual narrative, one that speaks to humanity's resilience and adaptability.

The cycles of nature and the symbolism they carried were so compelling that they later became intricately woven into the tapestry of Christian traditions.

While the sun no longer holds the central place in our idolatry that it once did, its legacy in holiday celebrations remains unmistakable, underscoring a shared human experience of anticipation and renewal that continues to resonate, even in our modern understandings of Christmas.

The Three-Day Sequence of the Sun's Death and Rebirth

Within the vast tapestry of winter solstice celebrations, a remarkable phenomenon centers around the perceived death and rebirth of the sun.

This period, closely observed by various ancient cultures, is characterized by the sun appearing to halt its southward journey for three days before it seemingly reverses course, promising the return of longer, warmer days. This natural occurrence has been laden with symbolic meaning, acting as a life-affirming harbinger of renewal and continuity.

Throughout history, the winter solstice marked a crucial point in the calendar, with many early societies regarding the sun's apparent stillness as a precursor to rebirth. During these three days, people participated in rituals to honor the sun's life cycle.

To ancient observers, the sun's pause on the horizon not only signified a period of reflection and gratitude for the past year's bounty, but also sparked hope for future growth and prosperity. The understanding and celebration of this cycle highlight humanity's enduring connection to the rhythms of nature.

Many spiritual traditions emphasized the sun as a symbol of light overcoming darkness, tying this celestial event to broader themes of death and resurrection. As cultures evolved, these motifs found echoes in various mythologies and religious narratives.

The winter solstice thus serves as a cornerstone of symbolic rebirth, weaving together the cycles of nature with human spirituality, impacting how communities perceived life and the afterlife.

In ancient times, the movements of the Sun held deep significance, guiding agricultural practices, religious rituals, and marking the seasons of life and survival.

Observers in the Northern Hemisphere noticed a fascinating celestial event each year around December 22nd: the Sun, which had been steadily moving lower in the sky as winter deepened, appeared to halt its descent.

This phenomenon (where the Sun seemed to pause and hover at the same spot along the horizon for three days) marked what was essentially a "standstill." During these three days, from December 22nd to December 24th, the Sun's position at dawn would remain fixed, not yet making its journey back up along the ecliptic. This cosmic pause gave the appearance that the Sun had symbolically "died."

On December 25th, the Sun would finally begin its subtle ascent, rising just one degree northward. To ancient eyes, this marked a powerful transition and was considered the "rebirth" of the Sun—a return from the symbolic death that preceded it.

It was a hopeful sign, symbolizing the coming of longer days and the eventual return of warmth, light, and growth.

This natural celestial event occurred near the "Crux constellation", also known as the Southern Cross, making it appear as though the Sun "died" on the cross during this standstill.

Thus, the three-day sequence of death and rebirth became a powerful symbol, giving rise to stories of resurrection tied to celestial movement.

The imagery of the Sun "dying" on the cross, remaining in a state of death for three days, and resurrecting on the third day has had enduring influence on human culture and spiritual traditions.

This cosmic drama represented not just the Sun's cyclical journey but a universal story of renewal, resilience, and hope.

As it ascended from this symbolic death, the Sun's rebirth foreshadowed the return of spring and life itself.

This annual cycle would find resonance in numerous religious narratives, intertwining the celestial and spiritual realms. For ancient civilizations, these events reflected an eternal truth—that darkness and decline are always followed by rebirth, a principle that would be woven into mythologies, teachings, and celebrations around the world.

I think it's important to note here that constellations shift over time due to what's known as the "precession of the equinoxes", and so the crux constellation is no longer in that vicinity (as seen from the northern hemisphere) as it has shifted over time but if you use astronomy software, you can run the clock back a few thousand years and see this very interesting phenomenon.

The precession of the equinoxes makes a complete cycle of the gradual shift in the Earth's rotational axis over approximately 26,000 years. This causes constellations to drift in position relative to Earth's horizon.

While the Crux constellation (known as the Southern Cross) was once visible in the vicinity of the Sun's southernmost point during winter solstice, it has since moved out of view from the Northern Hemisphere due to this slow shift.

In ancient times, when the Crux constellation was still visible to those in northern latitudes, it added to the symbolic story: the Sun appeared to "die" on the cross, pause for three days, and then "rise" or "resurrect" as it shifted northward.

Today, Crux or the Southern Cross is visible primarily from the Southern Hemisphere, but with modern astronomical software, we can rewind the celestial clock and observe the sky as it was thousands of years ago.

This allows us to witness the alignment and understand how ancient observers connected the Sun's standstill and rebirth with the nearby Crux constellation. This symbolic alignment, preserved through myth and astronomical knowledge, beautifully demonstrates how our ancestors observed, interpreted, and wove the cosmos into their cultural and spiritual traditions.

The entrancing three-day sequence of the sun's "death" and "rebirth" has shaped winter solstice celebrations across the ages, inspiring countless stories and practices that resonate with the essence of hope, transformation, and reawakening.

In these timeless observances, one finds a universal message of resilience and renewal, themes that continue to influence the cultural and religious traditions surrounding Christmas today.

Chapter 2:
Pagan Origins of Christmas

Christmas, as we know it, is a blend of diverse influences, many of which stem from ancient pagan traditions. It's a tapestry woven from threads of diverse cultures and beliefs.

The roots of these customs dig deep into early civilizations such as the Sumerians, Akkadians, and Babylonians. Their rituals, steeped in mystery and reverence for the natural world, provide a fascinating backdrop to the winter celebrations that would eventually blend into Christmas.

In these ancient cultures, the winter solstice marked a significant turning point—a time when the darkest days began to lengthen and light promised to return. This cosmic event was both celebrated and feared.

It's not surprising that sun worship played a vital role in these communities. The rebirth of the sun, symbolized through the return of longer days, mirrored human desires for resilience and renewal.

The Yule log, now associated with coziness and warmth, has its origins here too. Lighting a great fire on the longest night was a symbolic act of hope. It was believed to regenerate the sun's strength and invite prosperity for the coming year.

Such traditions highlighted the profound connection between humans and nature, a theme that resonates even now, as we gather around our firesides during the holiday season.

The influence of solar deities and their worship is a thread running through many pre-Christian traditions. Deities like Mithra and Sol Invictus personified the sun and were critical to these celebrations.

Observers of these gods would perform rituals designed to ensure the sun's return, painting the winter skies with bonfires and dances. As we look at how these practices wove their way into Christmas, it's hard not to see how inherently linked light and hope continue to be in this festive period.

Exploring Sumerian, Akkadian, and Babylonian Traditions

To truly dive into the pagan origins of Christmas, we must journey back in time to ancient Mesopotamia, where the Sumerians, Akkadians, and Babylonians held sway.

These civilizations, among the earliest in recorded history, laid down cultural practices that rippled across the ages, leaving a subtle yet profound imprint on what would eventually emerge as Christmas.

Their religious practices and mythologies intricately wove together natural phenomena and divine entities, creating a tapestry of traditions that are as fascinating as they are influential.

The Sumerians, with their advanced society, had stories centered around their pantheon of gods, who were intimately tied to celestial events. Central to their practice was the reverence of the sun and its cycles, much like numerous societies around the globe.

Their festivals marked the solar changes that later societies, including our own Christmas, would echo. The emphasis on light returning after lengthy darkness during the winter solstice can be traced back to these ancient narratives where themes of death and rebirth were prevalent.

Transitioning to the Akkadian era, the new kingdom assimilated many Sumerian practices, but they added their own layers of mythology. The sun god Shamash played a central role, embodying justice, truth, and bringing light to dark places.

His daily journey across the sky mirrored an ever-renewing battle against the encroaching night, a narrative that resonates in the heart of the Christmas season with its focus on light overcoming darkness.

Meanwhile, the Babylonians inherited and further developed these Sumerian-Akkadian traditions. They celebrated the festival of Zagmuk, a new year festival that coincided with the end of the winter solstice.

Zagmuk was a time of moral reversal and disorder, echoing the chaos of the dying year but heralding the birth of a new one. It's easy to see how these motifs of renewal and triumph over darkness seeped into the fibers of later winter celebrations, eventually merging into the Christmas tapestry.

Collectively, these ancient civilizations viewed the sun not just as a celestial body but as a divine force integral to the cosmos' cycle. Their impact reverberates through history, illustrating how deeply the past informs the present in the most unexpected ways.

Understanding this rich background enhances our comprehension of Christmas as not merely a modern holiday but as the culmination of millennia-old traditions that honor cycles of death and renewal, light, and dark.

Yule Log and New Fire Traditions

The ancient practice of lighting a Yule log during festivities finds its roots deep within the pagan traditions of Northern Europe.

This tradition, bursting with both symbolism and practicality, was one of many that underscored the pagan origins of what we now call Christmas. The act of setting a large log ablaze in the hearth served as an emblem of warmth and hope during the darkest days of winter, encapsulating the elemental struggle between light and dark.

It was more than just firewood; the Yule log was a beacon, a promise of the sun's eventual return after its long absence.

Yule, the Norse celebration of the winter solstice, marked a time of rest and reflection. People believed that burning a sizeable log over the twelve days of Yule would usher in good fortune and dispel the long shadows of the year past.

Communities would gather to carve runes and inscribe wishes on the log, infusing it with personal hopes and collective goodwill. As these flames danced, so did the spirits of those gathered, their hearts kindled by shared stories and ancient songs.

Parallel to these customs, the "new fire" traditions in various other cultures sought to renew life and vitality. The Celts, for instance, greeted the solstice by extinguishing old fires and kindling new ones, symbolizing purification and the vanquishing of past hardships.

This ritualistic renewal resonated with agricultural societies, who saw the solstice as a turning point in the wheel of the year—a bridge from the barrenness of winter to the burgeoning promise of spring.

As Christianity spread, these traditions seamlessly wove themselves into the fabric of Christmas celebrations. The endurance of the Yule log as a festive symbol is not merely nostalgia; it is a testament to the enduring power of ancient customs to adapt and endure in new contexts.

While the overt pagan connotations have receded into the backdrop, the core themes of light triumphing over darkness, and community ties strengthened around the fire, have remained intact, ever-present in the warmth and glow of the modern Christmas season.

The communal "new fire" ritual was a common, widespread and deeply rooted tradition across many ancient societies. This ritual, often symbolizing renewal, unity, and purification, was especially prominent around key seasonal transitions, marking both a spiritual and practical reset.

In addition to the Yule log rituals in Northern Europe, here's a closer look at how a "new fire" appeared across various cultures:

Celtic and Gaelic Traditions

Some ancient Celtic and Gaelic communities would extinguish all household fires on specific days of the year, often aligning with seasonal transitions or festivals like Samhain (October 31) or Imbolc (February 1).

A single communal fire would be kindled, and each family would take a flame back to rekindle their hearth, symbolizing unity and shared life force. While this wasn't January 1, the idea of collective renewal through fire was essential.

Roman and Greek Rituals

In ancient Rome, the festival of Vesta, goddess of the hearth, included rituals where the sacred fire was renewed. Similarly, Greek towns often had a central fire or altar in honor of Hestia, goddess of the hearth, kept alight year-round. Renewing the communal flame reinforced social unity and divine protection over the city.

Jewish and Early Christian Traditions

In Jewish tradition, the lighting of the menorah in the Temple symbolized a divine presence and continuity. Early Christian Easter customs involved lighting a Paschal candle to signify

Christ's resurrection, a new beginning, and the dispersion of darkness, often followed by individuals lighting their own candles from the communal flame.

Aztec New Fire Ceremony

The Aztecs of ancient Mexico performed a "new fire" ceremony every 52 years (their century cycle), where they would extinguish all fires, perform rituals, and light a new fire on January 1, symbolizing the start of a new cycle.

Every household would then take this new fire back home. Although not directly related to the Yule log, it is a famous tradition of "sharing a new fire" to symbolize renewal. This marked the renewal of the world for another cycle, symbolizing a rebirth for both the cosmos and society.

Hindu New Year

In various regions of India, Diwali and certain New Year festivals include lighting new lamps and candles to invite prosperity and dispel darkness. These rituals unite families and communities in marking an auspicious start to the year.

In fact, most of the world celebrated a "new fire" motif in one shape or fashion throughout the centuries that held similar significance. Each culture infused the ritual with its unique customs and meanings, but the core themes of renewal, unity, and purification remained consistent across these traditions.

China

In ancient China, fire held a prominent place in rituals, and fire altars were often used in ceremonies to honor ancestors and gods. The Chinese Lunar New Year and the Lantern Festival involve lighting lanterns and fireworks to "drive away evil spirits" and welcome prosperity.

During the Lunar New Year, it was also customary to clean the house and light new fires to signify a fresh start. Though not a "new fire" ritual in the strictest sense, these celebrations reinforce the concept of renewal and purification, marking a significant cultural reset.

Russia and Slavic Regions

In Russia and other Slavic lands, fire rituals were central to the festival of Kupala Night, celebrated around the summer solstice. During this festival, large bonfires would be lit, symbolizing purification and protection. People would often leap over the flames to drive away misfortune and bring luck.

For Slavic New Year traditions, fires were sometimes rekindled in honor of Sventovit (a god associated with fire and divination), as people sought blessings for the coming year.

Indigenous Siberian and Arctic Tribes

Indigenous Siberian groups, like the Yakuts, had ceremonies that incorporated the rekindling of flames in honor of sun spirits. Fire was believed to ward off the cold and bring warmth and life back into the frozen tundra. During spring and early summer festivals, communities would sometimes kindle new flames to signify the end of winter and a time of renewal.

The Chukchi and other Arctic tribes also had fire-based rituals where families and clans would gather to celebrate seasonal shifts, often rekindling flames in their communal areas to mark the new season.

Sub-Saharan Africa

Many Sub-Saharan African tribes, such as the Yoruba, have fire-centered ceremonies associated with their seasonal cycles and spiritual beliefs. In the Yoruba tradition, the lighting of new fires during festivals honors Shango, the god of thunder and lightning, who is closely associated with fire and renewal.

Across parts of East Africa, ceremonies involving the rekindling of fires are common during New Year or harvest festivals, symbolizing renewal and protection for the community.

Pacific Islands

In certain Pacific Island communities, fire rituals are tied to cultural festivals and agricultural cycles. For example, some Polynesian tribes held communal fires during the Makahiki season in Hawaii, a time dedicated to the god Lono, associated with peace and abundance.

Indigenous North American Tribes

Many Native American tribes have fire-centered ceremonies. The Hopi and Zuni peoples celebrate the winter solstice with fire as a representation of the sun's power. The Sunrise Ceremony is also important among various tribes, where fires are lit to greet the first light of the New Year, honoring a fresh cycle and new beginnings.

Ancient Near East (Mesopotamia, Sumer, Babylon)

In ancient Mesopotamia, fire was sacred and closely associated with gods like Nusku, the god of fire and light. While they didn't have a "new fire" tradition in the same sense, fire was used to mark the New Years festival, Akitu. Ritual fires in temples symbolized renewal and blessings for the coming year.

Indian Subcontinent

In India, the Lohri festival celebrated in Punjab (and Makar Sankranti across other regions) is centered around large bonfires lit in January, marking the end of winter and the sun's transition toward the Northern Hemisphere. Families gather around bonfires, symbolizing the burning of the old and the welcoming of the new.

In southern India, Karthika Deepam is a festival where lamps are lit to signify the triumph of light over darkness, and fires are kept burning to welcome prosperity and renewal.

Andean Cultures (Peru, Bolivia)

In the Andes, Inti Raymi (Festival of the Sun) is a winter solstice festival celebrated by the Inca and modern Quechua people. Although this occurs in June in the Southern Hemisphere, bonfires and ceremonial fires are an integral part of this tradition, marking the renewal of light and honoring Inti, the sun god.

Japan

In Japan, during the Obon Festival, fires known as mukaebi and okuribi are lit to guide ancestral spirits to and from the world of the living. While Obon centers on ancestors rather than a "new fire" specifically, it represents a similar theme of renewal and connection. Additionally, Kagami Biraki, held in January, includes breaking open sake barrels and lighting fires as a renewal ritual to start the year.

Korea

In Korea, fire-related rituals that echo the "new fire" concept, focusing on renewal and purification, are most prominent during "Jeongwol Daeboreum."

Jeongwol Daeboreum is a traditional Korean holiday celebrated on the first full moon of the lunar new year, usually falling in February. It marks a time of renewal, cleansing, and community well-being, embodying themes of health, prosperity, and protection for the year ahead.

"Jeongwol" means "first month," and "Daeboreum" means "great full moon," reflecting the timing of the celebration. During Jeongwol Daeboreum, several fire-related rituals and customs take place:

Daljip Taweugi (Burning of the Moon House): Daljip Taweugi is one of the most iconic rituals involves building a large bonfire called the *daljip* or "moon house," usually constructed from straw or branches. Villagers gather to light it, symbolically burning away misfortune and ushering in good fortune. As the *daljip* burns, people make wishes for health, happiness, and bountiful harvests in the coming year.

This ritual, held on the first full moon of the lunar new year, is meant to drive away evil spirits and bring good fortune for the year ahead. Watching the flames rise is believed to symbolize purification and the community's collective renewal.

Jwibulnori (Field Burning for a New Harvest): In agricultural communities, children and adults carry torches or straw bundles, walking around rice paddies or fields and setting the ground ablaze. This controlled burning helps eliminate pests and fertilizes the soil in preparation for new growth.

During Jeongwol Daeboreum, Jwibulnori is performed, where villagers light cans filled with burning embers and swing them over fields. The embers help to burn away old grass, pests, and disease from the previous season, ensuring a fresh and fertile environment for new crops. This agricultural practice has both practical and symbolic significance, embodying the themes of cleansing and new beginnings.

Each of these examples showcases how the concept of "new fire" rituals transcends geography and specific customs. These rituals underscore a shared human reverence for fire as both a physical and spiritual force, with flames representing the light of new beginnings and the strength of community bonds across diverse cultural landscapes.

These rituals emphasize a communal approach to renewal, with fire as the medium through which past energies are cleared to welcome a prosperous and harmonious year. They typically mark a ceremonial start to the season, symbolizing cleansing and fertility, and were often the basis of community-wide celebrations and dances.

This common motif reflects a universal human connection to fire as a life-giving and sacred force. By renewing the flame communally, ancient societies reinforced bonds between people and with the divine, collectively embracing hope and transformation. The enduring symbolism has carried into modern celebrations, reminding us of our shared heritage and humanity.

These ritual fires across different cultures highlight humanity's long-standing reverence for fire as a powerful symbol of renewal, hope, and transformation—elements that easily found their way into the Christmas story.

The Yule log, communal bonfires, and other "new fire" traditions resonate with core Christmas themes of light overcoming darkness and the promise of rebirth during winter's bleakest days.

These rituals signify continuity and connection to nature's cycles, mirroring how the Christmas story also celebrates renewal and togetherness. Just as the Yule log in Europe and other new fire practices symbolized the sun's eventual return, these elements were naturally incorporated into Christmas customs, blending spiritual beliefs with celebrations of family and community.

The fire traditions—from the Yule log's hearthside warmth to the large communal fires of Jeongwol Daeboreum—link ancient practices with the comforting glow of modern Christmas festivities.

Influence of Solar Deities and Sun Worship in Christmas

As we delve into the rich tapestry of traditions that shape Christmas, an illuminating thread reveals itself in the influence of solar deities and the ancient practice of sun worship.

This connection isn't just a footnote in history; it's a fascinating part of the story that shows how human cultures have long intertwined the cosmic movements with their most cherished festivities.

The winter solstice, celebrated across many cultures as a time of rebirth and renewal, naturally aligns with the awe humans have historically felt toward the sun. For centuries, civilizations saw the sun's annual cycle as a divine narrative, and their deities often mirrored this celestial journey.

Deities like Ra of the Egyptians, Helios of the Greeks, and Sol of the Romans held prominent roles as patrons of the sun, each influencing human behavior and rituals.

In the Roman world, the worship of Sol Invictus ("Unconquered Sun") gained prominence, especially after becoming associated with the emperor Constantine's rule.

Celebrated on December 25th, the feast of Sol Invictus coincided with the Natalis Invicti, a festival honoring the new sun after the solstice. This choice wasn't arbitrary; it symbolized the sun's shift from its lowest point back to ascendancy, a metaphor of triumph over darkness that resonated with the cultural psyche.

As Christianity began to weave itself into the Roman cultural fabric, these solar motifs didn't simply disappear but instead morphed and merged, contributing to the symbolic tapestry of Christmas.

The choice of December 25th as the date to celebrate Christ's birth can be seen not just as a strategic move for ease of conversion but also as a reflection of the symbolic rebirth theme that both the sun's return and Christ shared.

This blending of traditions wasn't just political sleight of hand; it served a deeper purpose in the spiritual landscape. The parallels between the newly born sun and the birth of a Savior fostered a sense of continuity for converts.

It provided a seamless transition from the old faiths to the new, where the light of understanding and hope literally and figuratively grew stronger with each passing day after the solstice.

The legacy of these ancient solar celebrations remains etched into the modern-day Christmas ethos. It's a testament to how human cultures reflect and adapt to the natural world, drawing upon its rhythms to craft a narrative of hope, renewal, and shared experience.

This interplay between pagan and Christian practices underlines how the strands of different beliefs often become part of a single, beautiful fabric that continues to cloak our festive traditions.

Chapter 3:
The Adaptation of Pagan Traditions

The integration of pagan traditions into early Christian practices wasn't a straightforward process. It involved a complex dance between old and new, blending rituals that had stood the test of time with emerging Christian customs.

This merging of traditions was often driven by practicality and necessity rather than spiritual coherence. When Christianity began to spread across Europe, it encountered deeply rooted pagan customs that couldn't simply be eradicated. Instead, these practices were skillfully woven into the fabric of a growing Christian identity.

At the heart of this adaptation was the political and religious landscape of the Roman Empire. Under emperors like Constantine and Theodosius, there was a clear push to unite the empire under a single faith.

To achieve this, they recognized the need to adapt existing pagan rituals to fit Christian narratives. This approach not only eased the transition for converts but also helped consolidate their power over a diverse population.

The church, with its growing influence, played a crucial role in redefining pagan customs, repurposing them with Christian symbolism. This strategic syncretism created a more palatable form of Christianity that could be embraced by former pagans.

Local traditions also found a way into the burgeoning Christmas celebrations. In various regions, communities clung to their ancestral customs, resulting in a tapestry of diverse practices under the umbrella of Christmas.

From the lighting of candles to the use of evergreens, many elements have their roots in pre-Christian winter solstice festivities. These cultural influences enriched the holiday, adding layers of meaning and history.

The adaptation of pagan traditions into Christmas wasn't just about bridging new and old worlds; it was about creating a holiday filled with shared symbols and communal rituals, ensuring its appeal to a wider audience through time.

Integration into Early Christian Practices

As Christianity began to spread through the Roman Empire, it found itself in a unique position of both competition and collaboration with existing pagan traditions.

To endure and expand, early Christians had to smartly incorporate elements of popular pagan practices into their own rituals, offering a seamless transition for converts and blending old customs with new beliefs.

During these early centuries, the Church faced the challenge of standing out while absorbing the familiar. Traditional Roman festivals like Saturnalia, with its feasting, merry-making, and gift-giving, were deeply rooted in the cultural psyche.

These festivities occurred around the same time as the fledgling Christian celebration of the birth of Jesus. The Church saw an opportunity—a chance to co-opt these rituals, providing a sense of continuity for new Christians while embedding the significance of Christ's birth into the cultural calendar.

One particular strategy was the adaptation of the winter solstice celebrations, an important time for many pagan cultures, symbolizing the death and rebirth of the sun.

To many early Christians, this parallel of rebirth resonated deeply with the nativity story, allowing for a theological interpretation whereby the birth of Christ would metaphorically herald the rebirth of the world.

This blending extended beyond mere symbolism. Church leaders like Pope Julius I formalized December 25th as the official date to observe Christ's birth. This strategic move aligned perfectly with the existing pagan celebrations around the winter solstice, creating a hybrid holiday that appealed to both Christians and those lingering in pagan traditions.

The process wasn't solely about dates and festivities; it involved a nuanced, calculated integration of rites and symbols that enabled Christianity to weave itself into the fabric of daily life.

By rebranding these existing customs into a Christian context, early Church leaders effectively used a syncretic approach—the blending of different religious beliefs and practices—to ensure the conversion of entire communities felt less like a cultural upheaval and more like a natural evolution.

This strategy of adaptation didn't just help Christianity grow; it also enriched the faith itself, adding layers of cultural depth and tradition that continue to be explored and celebrated today.

As we see, what might appear as a straightforward celebration of Jesus' birth is, in fact, the result of centuries of thoughtful transformation, tailored to unite a diverse body of believers under a shared, festive banner.

The Role of Church and Politics in Christmas Development

As Christmas emerged from its pagan roots, the role of the Church and political leaders became crucial in shaping the holiday as we know it today.

Initially, this transformation wasn't a simple matter of renouncing old ways but rather a complex integration of existing beliefs and customs into Christian ideology. This adaptation was both strategic and pragmatic, driven by the Church's need to establish a unified religious framework in a diverse Roman Empire.

During the reign of Emperor Constantine, who notably converted to Christianity, there was a pronounced shift towards adopting and adapting traditions that were familiar to the populace.

For Constantine, integrating festive elements of Saturnalia, a popular Roman festival, into Christian celebrations served a dual purpose. It eased the transition for newly converted Christians and also reinforced his political strategy of centralizing power under one faith.

The choice of December 25th as the date to celebrate the birth of Christ was also not coincidental. It conveniently aligned with Saturnalia and the birth of Sol Invictus, a date marked by widespread festivity throughout the empire.

Theodosius, who later declared Christianity the official religion of the Roman Empire, further entrenched this synthesis of traditions. By this time, the Church had recognized the persuasive power of the familiar.

Rather than abolishing deeply-rooted customs, the Church sought to reframe them within a Christian context. This process of syncretism was pivotal in winning over the hearts and minds of the populace, who found comfort in maintaining cultural traditions, albeit under a new religious guise.

The political machinations of this era also played a significant role. As rulers like Constantine and Theodosius used religion as a stabilizing force in governance, the Church seized opportunities to align itself with temporal power.

This alliance allowed Christian leaders to shape public policy and wield influence over cultural practices. It was a marriage of convenience wherein both the state and the Church benefitted—from increased control and broader acceptance, respectively.

In summary, the transformation of Christmas from its pagan origins into a cornerstone of Christian tradition wasn't merely a religious affair; it was deeply embedded in the political ambitions of the era.

By smartly weaving together elements of pagan revelry with the spiritual narrative of Christ's birth, Church and state created a holiday that was both inclusive and doctrinally robust, setting the stage for the rich tapestry of Christmas traditions that would continue to evolve across centuries.

Constantine, Theodosius, and Empire Christianization

The political context of the time played an instrumental role in the transformation of Christmas from a diverse array of pagan practices into a unified Christian celebration.

In the early stages of the Roman Empire's embrace of Christianity, pivotal leaders like Constantine and Theodosius were at the forefront, orchestrating a grand fusion of politics, religion, and cultural traditions. They effectively used their political clout to promote Christianity, reshaping the empire's religious landscape and paving the way for Christmas as we recognize it today.

Constantine's conversion to Christianity marked a significant turning point. As the first Roman Emperor to convert, he not only legitimized the faith but also laid the groundwork for its spread throughout the empire.

Under his rule, Christianity began to intertwine more visibly with Roman traditions. This wasn't just about religious observance; it was a shrewd political maneuver.

By blending Christian and pagan elements, Constantine maintained the cohesion and stability of an empire teeming with a mosaic of beliefs. It's under his reign that we see early traces of Christmas traditions borrowed from winter solstice celebrations, which were fundamentally pagan in nature.

Theodosius took this transformation further, making Christianity the official state religion of the Roman Empire. With this decree came an increased focus on differentiating Christian practices, such as Christmas, from their pagan predecessors.

Nevertheless, the transition wasn't abrupt or absolute. It involved strategic adaptation and inclusion of familiar customs to ensure that Christianity could accommodate the empire's diverse populace. As Christmas evolved, it borrowed liberally from existing celebrations like Saturnalia, satisfying a cultural need while reinforcing theological messages.

Through these political actions, Constantine and Theodosius weren't merely shaping religious observance; they were navigating the art of governance through religious inclusivity and unity.

This skillful blending not only solidified Christianity's dominion but also ensured that the essence of certain pagan traditions survived, albeit reborn under a new guise. Thus, the political initiatives of these emperors didn't just Christianize an empire—they reshaped the very fabric of cultural celebration, embedding Christmas with a rich, multifaceted heritage.

Syncretism and Local Traditions in Christmas

Christmas, as we know it today, is a tapestry woven with threads from a diverse array of cultural and religious practices. The process of syncretism (where different traditions blend and evolve into something new) has played a pivotal role in shaping these celebrations.

As Christianity spread, early Christians found themselves amidst a myriad of pre-existing pagan rituals and customs, and it was this interplay that led to the unique character of Christmas.

In many regions, local traditions met with Christian beliefs, resulting in a festival that resonated with both ancient and contemporary elements. This meeting of the old and new didn't happen in isolation but through a subtle yet significant negotiation of meanings.

In many parts of Europe, for example, midwinter festivals that once celebrated the winter solstice were reinterpreted as Christmas celebrations. The celebration of light overcoming darkness (a central theme in many solstice festivities) mirrored the Christian belief in the birth of Christ as a symbol of hope and salvation.

Given the vast diversity of cultures across Europe and other regions, the adoption and adaptation of pagan customs couldn't help but vary. In Scandinavia, the Yule traditions brought along customs like the Yule log, which became intertwined with Christmas lore.

Meanwhile, in Italy, ancient Roman influences found their way into Christmas through the remnants of Saturnalia festivities, a time once marked by merriment, gift-giving, and communal feasting. This ability to adapt local traditions into the broader Christian narrative ensured an easier acceptance of Christmas across different cultures and, importantly, maintained a connection to the community's heritage.

The role of the church in this syncretism cannot be overstated. Rather than eradicating cherished local customs, ecclesiastical leaders often sought to reinterpret and Christianize them.

This strategy not only helped facilitate the spread of Christianity but also enriched the cultural fabric of Christmas.

As local folklore merged with religious observance, new traditions emerged, offering a richer, more inclusive celebration that could unify rather than divide.

Interestingly, the syncretism of Christmas traditions was not a uniform process and varied greatly depending on political, geographical, and cultural factors. Some regions clung more tightly to their pagan roots, while others embraced new Christian customs more readily.

The adaptation of these traditions highlights the complexity of cultural evolution and demonstrates how, over time, Christmas has grown into a holiday that is both deeply rooted in the past and ever-evolving.

The beauty of syncretism in Christmas lies in its flexibility—the ability to maintain ancient customs while embracing new interpretations. These blended traditions form a celebration that resonates with people across different backgrounds and beliefs, making Christmas a truly global festival.

Cultural Influences on Christmas Traditions

When we think of Christmas, images of twinkling lights, decorated evergreens, and festive gatherings come to mind. But the origins of these beloved customs are a rich tapestry of cultural influences, woven together through centuries of adaptation.

At the heart of these traditions lies the intricate blending of pagan rites with emerging Christian practices, all shaped dramatically by a myriad of cultural forces.

The transformation didn't happen overnight. As Christianity spread across Europe, it encountered a patchwork of pagan traditions deeply rooted in local customs and beliefs.

These indigenous festivals, often linked to the turning of the seasons, offered natural alignments with the themes of

Christmas like light in darkness, renewal, and hope. The Church, recognizing the potential for religious syncretism, gradually began to incorporate these practices into the fabric of Christian worship.

Take, for instance, the influence of Norse traditions. The Yule festivities, marked by the burning of the Yule log to summon the sun's return, found their way into Christmas through Northern European customs.

Over time, the grand Yule celebrations became intertwined with Christmas observances, bringing with them a sense of warmth and togetherness during the coldest, darkest time of the year.

In fact, we still sing traditional Christmas carols that reflect the Yule log and its symbolism. The song **Deck the Halls** is one of the best-known examples, with lyrics like "*See the blazing Yule before us, fa la la la la, la la la la.*" This line celebrates the Yule log burning brightly as a central part of the festive season.

The Yule log's presence in songs like this keeps the spirit of ancient winter solstice traditions alive, connecting the warmth and light of the Yule log to the joy and comfort that Christmas brings today. It's a reminder of how these ancient symbols continue to warm our modern celebrations.

What about, **The Christmas Song** ("*Chestnuts roasting on an open fire, Yuletide carols being sung by a choir*"), also speaks to the tradition of celebrating and singing about the season of Yule.

Meanwhile, in the British Isles, the reverence for evergreen plants such as holly and ivy was prominent in pre-Christian winter rites. These plants, symbolic of eternal life, were soon absorbed into Christmas decorations, carrying with them their pagan significance while contributing to the visual language of the holiday.

In contrast, the Mediterranean region shaped Christmas through an entirely different cultural lens. Roman traditions like Saturnalia and the feast of Sol Invictus left indelible marks on Christmas celebrations. The jubilant public revelries and exchanges of gifts during these festivals influenced the convivial nature of Christmas, embedding a sense of community and shared joy.

Cultural influences didn't stop with the dawn of Christianity, nor did they remain confined to Europe. With the advent of exploration and colonization, Christmas traditions began to reflect a broader mosaic of global customs. In places like Latin America, indigenous and colonial influences melded with European Christmas practices, resulting in unique and vibrant celebrations.

Each of these cultural layers added new colors and textures to Christmas, allowing the holiday to be both personal and universal. As we celebrate today, these historical threads remind us of a shared human experience—one that transforms and evolves, yet always, in essence, seeks light in the darkest of times.

Chapter 4:
The Role of Saint Nicholas

As we delve into the transformation of Christmas over the centuries, a key figure stands out: Saint Nicholas. This historical figure, renowned for his generosity and kindness, became an enduring symbol in the tapestry of Christmas traditions.

Born in the third century in the town of Patara (modern-day Turkey), Nicholas was deeply revered for his piety and goodwill, often helping those in desperate need. These acts of kindness gradually spun into numerous legends and tales, painting him as a benefactor of children and protector of sailors.

Saint Nicholas' transformation from a revered saint to the jolly figure of Santa Claus is a fascinating journey. The tale doesn't just leap across countries; it morphs through time, reflecting societal changes and cultural exchanges.

The Dutch played a critical role in this metamorphosis, celebrating "Sinterklaas" with a jovial spirit and traditional fervor. When Dutch settlers brought the legend of Sinterklaas to America, the adaptation started in earnest, blending folklore with New World ideas to create what we now recognize as Santa Claus.

The imagery and attributes we associate with Santa—his red suit, affinity for chimneys, and sleigh pulled by reindeer—were not born overnight. Instead, they were painted onto the canvas of Christmas lore through a combination of poem, prose, and commercial interests.

Clement Clarke Moore's poem "A Visit from St. Nicholas" was instrumental in sculpting Santa's modern persona. This poem, along with illustrations from the likes of Thomas Nast, etched Santa into the public consciousness.

By exploring the evolution of Saint Nicholas, we can see how deeply intertwined this transformation is with the broader cultural evolution of Christmas. It's a testament to how traditions endure by adapting to the times, drawing from historical roots while branching into the new.

Saint Nicholas, both in his quiet acts of generosity and his loud, joyful celebrations as Santa Claus, symbolizes the enduring spirit of giving and joy that continues to define the holiday season.

Historical Figure of Saint Nicholas

The tale of Saint Nicholas, nestled in the annals of history, offers a glimpse into the complex tapestry of Christian and pre-Christian traditions that influence modern-day Christmas.

Born around 270 AD in the ancient town of Patara, located in present-day Turkey, Nicholas was a man of profound generosity and unyielding faith. He grew up in a wealthy family, yet he chose to dedicate his life to the service of the less fortunate, a choice that would cement his legacy for generations.

As the Bishop of Myra, Nicholas became famed for his acts of kindness and miraculous deeds. The tales of his benevolence are myriad, with one of the most popular being his discreet gift-giving to save three sisters from a life of destitution.

He'd allegedly drop bags of gold into their home under the cover of darkness, thereby establishing the poetic roots for the custom of secret gift-giving we cherish today.

But Nicholas' story didn't merely end in the quiet streets of Myra. His popularity burgeoned after his death, with countless miracles attributed to his intercession.

As his veneration spread, he became known as the protector of sailors, children, and the destitute. His feast day, December 6th, was widely celebrated across Europe, especially in the Netherlands, where he became "Sinterklaas."

Saint Nicholas, aka Sinterklaas, a cherished figure depicted as an elderly, bishop-like man with a flowing white beard, red robes, and a mitre (a tall headdress worn by bishops), often riding a white horse.

Traditionally, Sinterklaas arrives by ship from Spain in mid-November, kicking off a season of celebration. Accompanied by his helpers known as Zwarte Piet (Black Peter), he visits towns across the country, giving small gifts and sweets to children. Children place shoes by the fireplace or door, filled with hay or carrots for his horse, in hopes of receiving treats in return.

This celebration has long been one of the most anticipated events in the Dutch festive season, with its own customs, songs, and symbols. Sinterklaas embodies the spirit of kindness and generosity that was attributed to the original Saint Nicholas, but his character is shaped by Dutch customs and sensibilities.

It's fascinating how deeply Nicholas' narrative intertwines with cultural evolution, eventually morphing into the modern mythology of Santa Claus.

From medieval celebrations that honored his piety and charity to the secular traditions observed across the globe today, Saint Nicholas stands as a pillar in the intricate evolution of Christmas, bridging the gap between historical reverence and contemporary charm.

Understanding the life and legend of Saint Nicholas offers a key to unlocking the complex metamorphosis of joyous traditions into the festive season as we know it. His undying legacy of generosity, merged with folklore and cultural adaptation, underscores the profound impact one historical figure can have on shaping an enduring holiday narrative.

Transformation to Sinterklaas and Santa Claus

The transition from the saintly Bishop of Myra to the jolly figure cherished worldwide as Santa Claus is a fascinating journey through time, culture, and imagination.

It began with the historical figure of Saint Nicholas, a 4th-century bishop renowned for his generosity, particularly towards children and the poor. His acts of kindness and selflessness became legendary, inspiring communities far beyond his homeland.

As the centuries passed, the story of Saint Nicholas traveled across Europe, gaining new shades and characteristics. In the Netherlands, he transformed into Sinterklaas, a beloved figure who arrived by ship from Spain, riding a white horse and carrying gifts for children.

Dutch traditions celebrated Sinterklaas on the evening of December 5th, with children leaving **shoes** out to be filled with candies and gifts.

When Dutch settlers voyaged to America in the 17th century, they brought their traditions with them. The imagery of Sinterklaas mingled with local folklore and the influence of other cultures, giving rise to a uniquely American character.

By the 19th century, the name Santa Claus emerged, echoing the phonetics of its Dutch predecessor. Over time, American culture added its own embellishments to Santa's persona.

The iconic image of a plump, jolly old man, dressed in a red suit and traveling the world in a reindeer-drawn sleigh, owes much to contributors like Clement Clarke Moore and the illustrations of Thomas Nast.

This blend of old-world charm with new-world creativity solidified Santa's role in the collective consciousness, becoming as essential to the Christmas experience as the holiday itself.

Thus, the transformation from Saint Nicholas to Sinterklaas and finally to Santa Claus not only reflects a cultural evolution but also a testament to the persistent and adaptable spirit of Christmas traditions across different societies.

Each iteration of this iconic figure resonates with its own time and place, yet all stay true to the core virtues of generosity and joy that started it all.

How Saint Nicholas Became Santa Claus

The journey from Saint Nicholas to Santa Claus is as winding as a snow-covered forest path.

As mentioned earlier, it all began with a 4th-century Greek bishop named Nicholas, known for his generosity and miracle-working. This historical figure became a saintly icon in both Eastern and Western Christianity, revered for his acts of kindness and his legendary secret gift-giving to those in need.

As centuries rolled on, the legacy of Saint Nicholas morphed, shaped by the cultural winds blowing across Europe. The Dutch played an important role in this transformation. They brought with them to America stories of 'Sinterklaas,' an adaptation of Saint Nicholas, when they settled in what is now known as New York.

Sinterklaas was a bishop-like figure donning red robes and a tall, brimmed hat, who would travel on a white horse delivering gifts to well-behaved children. It's fascinating to see how oral legends and family traditions helped underpin Saint Nicholas's character into something new on foreign soil.

When Dutch settlers brought their traditions to the American colonies, they introduced the figure of Sinterklaas to their new home. Over time, this Dutch saint morphed through various influences, merging with other folk figures and evolving in character and appearance.

The name "Sinterklaas" was Anglicized to Santa Claus, and he gradually lost his bishop's attire, mitre, and horse. The figure of Santa Claus further evolved in American popular culture, thanks to the contributions of various artists, writers, and marketers.

In the melting pot of the New World, the tale of Sinterklaas continued to evolve. One writer named, Washington Irving wrote about St. Nicholas in a book titled, *A History of New York* (published in 1809 under the pseudonym Diedrich Knickerbocker).

Here, Irving described St. Nicholas as a jolly Dutch figure who would ride over rooftops in a wagon, a concept that influenced the later depiction of Santa Claus.

One significant step in this transformation was the poem "*A Visit from St. Nicholas*" (commonly known as *'Twas the Night Before Christmas*) by Clement Clarke Moore in 1823.

This poem (written for his children) introduced the image of Santa Claus as a "right jolly old elf" with a sleigh pulled by reindeer, a departure from the solemn Sinterklaas of the Netherlands.

Later, artist Thomas Nast illustrated Santa as a plump, bearded man in a red suit in the late 1800s, cementing this image in the public mind.

Their works painted a new image, showing a cheerful, plump, pipe-smoking Santa sliding down chimneys with reindeer and a sleigh. This newly minted Santa Claus veered away from his solemn ecclesiastical roots, taking on a more whimsical and magical persona, a perfect fit for the more secular and commercial aspects of Christmas that were emerging.

The mythos was further enriched over the years through literature, media, and marketing campaigns. Notably, the Coca-Cola Company's advertising in the 1930s brought the modern, jolly Santa—complete with his iconic red suit trimmed with white fur—vividly into the public consciousness.

This imagery was instrumental in establishing Santa's role as a central figure in Christmas celebrations worldwide, embodying the spirit of giving and joy.

Santa Claus, Saint Nicholas took on a new identity in the United States, adopting characteristics suited to American ideals of the time (a more casual and merry figure), focused on joy, warmth, and inclusivity.

With the commercial rise of Christmas in the 20th century, Santa Claus became a central icon, not just of gift-giving, but also of family gatherings, community, and goodwill.

Today, Sinterklaas and Santa Claus coexist as distinct yet related figures. In the Netherlands and Belgium, Sinterklaas is still celebrated with many of the original customs, marking a separate day from Christmas and retaining his saintly character.

Meanwhile, in much of the world, Santa Claus is the star of Christmas Eve, embodying the spirit of giving that transcends cultural and religious boundaries. The journey from Saint Nicholas to Sinterklaas to Santa Claus reflects a fascinating blend of tradition and innovation, showing how cultural figures evolve to resonate with each generation.

So, as we unwrap the tale of how Saint Nicholas became Santa Claus, we find a story woven from cultural exchanges, poetic license, and commercial influence.

This transformation reflects broader themes of adaptation and syncretism that have shaped Christmas' evolution, revealing how traditions can blend and adapt to suit the times and places they inhabit.

Chapter 5:
Christmas as a Christian Holiday

As Christianity began to spread across the Roman Empire, the church faced the challenge of integrating diverse cultures and their traditions.

Early Christians, seeking to differentiate their practices from paganism while still appealing to converts, began to reimagine various elements of existing celebrations. One significant endeavor was the rebranding of the midwinter festivities into a distinctly Christian holiday. By reinterpreting and adapting earlier customs, the Church sought to establish a new religious narrative centered on the birth of Jesus Christ.

The decision to celebrate Christmas on December 25th was not by accident. It coincides with existing pagan celebrations like the Roman Saturnalia and Sol Invictus, which celebrated the rebirth of the sun.

By choosing this date, the Church skillfully aligned the event with a period already marked by festivity and renewal, easing the transition for those familiar with the pagan calendar. This clever synchronization not only aided in conversion but also helped to unify the Christian community during a time of spiritual reflection and communal joy.

Throughout the medieval period, Christmas continued to evolve. It took on layers of mythological syncretism, with stories and characters from various cultures blending into the Christian narrative.

During this era, the church skillfully adopted popular stories, weaving them into celebrations, reflecting humanity's talent for spreading ideas as readily as territories.

The celebration of the nativity, with its unique blend of sacred rituals and borrowed folkloric elements, became a time for both solemn worship and joyous feasting.

The Christian Reformation brought its own set of challenges and transformations to Christmas celebrations. Protestant reformers questioned and sometimes rejected the Catholic Church's established traditions.

Yet, despite such conflicts, the core of Christmas as a recognition of Christ's birth remained. It became a moment for communities to reaffirm their faith and find unity in shared beliefs, proving once again the resilience and adaptability of this cherished holiday.

Early Christian Rebranding of Christmas

As Christianity took root in the Roman Empire, the leaders of the early Church faced a daunting challenge: how to integrate this new faith into a world steeped in pagan traditions.

One of the most strategic moves was the rebranding of existing winter solstice celebrations into a distinctly Christian holiday. This wasn't simply a spiritual decision but a calculated effort to ease the transition for converts by infusing familiar seasonal rites with Christian meaning.

Winter solstice festivals, filled with themes of light and renewal, were ripe for adaptation. As the longest night of the year passed and the days began to lengthen, people celebrated the return of the sun.

For early Christians, this solstice symbolism could naturally align with the birth of Christ, "**the light of the world.**"

It was a brilliant stroke of theological adaptation, allowing the celebration of Jesus' nativity to resonate with the established rhythm of life.

By the way, there are numerous metaphors and titles comparing Jesus to the sun, many of which have deep roots in early Christian and pre-Christian traditions that align with celestial imagery. Here are some common ones:

1. *Light of the World* – *(John 8:12)* *"*I am the light of the world. Whoever follows me will never walk in darkness, but will have the light of life.*" Signifying Jesus as a guiding light, like the sun that illuminates the day.*

2. **The Risen Savior** – Paralleling the sun's daily rise, symbolizing Jesus' resurrection and the triumph over darkness.

3. **The Sun of Righteousness** – Found in the Old Testament (Malachi 4:2) and linked to Jesus in Christian tradition, emphasizing warmth, healing, and purity.

4. **The Eternal Light** – (John 8:12, Psalm 27:1, John 1:4-5, 1 John 1:5) Reflecting the never-ending brightness of the sun and the promise of eternal guidance by Jesus.

5. **The Light of Life** (John 8:12, John 1:4) Highlighting Jesus as a source of spiritual life, just as the sun sustains earthly life.

6. **The True Light** (John 1:9) *"The true light that gives light to everyone was coming into the world."* This captures the imagery of Jesus as divine, akin to the heavenly body that lights up our world.

7. *The Radiant One (Hebrews 1:3)* *"*The Son is the radiance of God's glory and the exact representation of his being, sustaining all things by his powerful word.*"*

8. **Crown of Thorns** – (Matthew 27:29) Often likened to sun rays, as seen in artistic depictions where Jesus'

crown resembles radiant light or a halo, emphasizing divinity and enlightenment.

9. **The Alpha and Omega** (Revelation 22:13) "I am the Alpha and the Omega, the First and the Last, the Beginning and the End." *Explanation:* Jesus as the eternal beginning and end, similar to the sun marking the start and close of each day.

10. **Redeemer** *(*Isaiah 60:1) "Arise, shine, for your light has come, and the glory of the Lord rises upon you." *Explanation:* Jesus as redeemer brings light to those in spiritual darkness, much like the sun rising after night.

Each of these metaphors capture different aspects of Jesus' role in Christian theology while emphasizing qualities commonly associated with the sun: life-giving, unwavering, and illuminating. They showcase a blend of spiritual symbolism and the natural world's enduring imagery.

When Was Jesus Actually Born?

December 25th was chosen by the early Catholic Church in the 4th century as a way to align Jesus' birth celebration with existing Roman and pagan winter solstice festivals, such as the celebration of Sol Invictus, the "Unconquered Sun."

This adaptation helped early Christianity grow by aligning with well-established celebrations and creating a new significance around Jesus as the "light of the world."

Based on clues from the Gospel narratives, most theories about the timing of Jesus' birth point to spring or early fall.

So while most Christians celebrate the birth of Christ on December 25th, many believe that Jesus' actual birth likely took place during warmer months.

By claiming this day for a new Christian purpose, the Church could draw pagans into the fold by preserving the festivity and communal spirit already associated with the time of year.

Moreover, the rebranding of Christmas was a tool for unification within the growing Christian community. Emerging out of a myriad of local traditions and beliefs, this cohesive celebration helped bind the faithful to a common spiritual identity.

The Church's establishment of a Christ-centered festival at the winter solstice turned the tide in favor of Christianity, both smoothing the path for conversion and asserting the religion's growing cultural prominence.

This strategic reimagining illustrates the early Church's perceptive insight into human nature and cultural dynamics. By overlaying Christian narratives onto deeply rooted traditions, they not only honored the past but set a powerful precedent for the future evolution of Christmas. What emerged was a celebration that, while inherently Christian at its core, still echoed the ancient rhythms and imagery of a world in transition.

Establishment of December 25th as Christmas

The choice of December 25th as the date to celebrate Christmas wasn't merely a random decision, but rather a carefully orchestrated move influenced by religious, cultural, and political factors.

In the early centuries of Christianity, there was no unanimous agreement on when to celebrate the birth of Jesus Christ. Different regions observed this pivotal event on different dates, if at all. The lack of a standardized date reflects not only the infancy of the Church's structure but also the intertwining of various cultural influences that shaped early Christian practices.

In Rome, this date coincided with Saturnalia, a popular festival celebrating the agricultural god Saturn, marked by feasting, gift-giving, and merrymaking. Another significant celebration around this time was the Dies Natalis Solis Invicti, the birthday of the unconquered sun, a festival honoring the sun god Sol Invictus.

By establishing December 25th as Christ's mass, the Church could integrate these widely observed pagan traditions into the Christian calendar, facilitating a smoother transition and conversion of the pagan population.

Furthermore, theological reasoning played a role in the decision. Early Christian theorists sought to draw symbolic parallels between Jesus and the sun, both heralding salvation and enlightenment.

They saw Christ as the "light of the world," mirroring the sun's rebirth after the winter solstice, when the days begin to lengthen again. This alignment provided a strong, symbolic narrative that Jesus' birth marked the dawn of a new era for humanity, a time when light would conquer darkness.

The political aspect shouldn't be overlooked either. The unification of the Roman Empire under a single religion was an ambitious project, and Emperor Constantine's conversion to Christianity facilitated this monumental shift.

By selecting December 25th, the Church capitalized on existing traditions to ease the empire's transition towards a unified Christian observance, reinforcing the empire's cohesion under a singular religious banner.

The Three Kings

One curious anomaly to point out is that of "the Three Kings" are said to have followed the bright star in the East to locate the birth of the savior.

The Bible recounts the story of the wise men, often referred to as the "three kings," following a star in the east to find the newborn Jesus in the Gospel of Matthew (Matthew 2:1-12).

However the Bible doesn't specify that there were three kings—only that they were "wise men from the east." The tradition of "three kings" likely arose because of the three gifts they presented: gold, frankincense, and myrrh.

In Matthew 2:2, the wise men arrive in Jerusalem and ask, "Where is he who has been born king of the Jews? For we saw his star when it rose and have come to worship him."

This "star in the east" (sometimes called the "Star of Bethlehem") is what allegedly guided them toward Jesus. The wise men continued to follow the star, which "*went ahead of them until it stopped over the place where the child was*" (Matthew 2:9).

The interpretation here has fascinated scholars and theologians for centuries, as it suggests a bright, moving star that led them to a specific location. Some suggest it could have been a comet, a supernatural event, or even an alien spacecraft.

The star has long been interpreted as a symbol of divine guidance. To the Magi, who were likely astrologers or astronomers from Persia, it would have been a significant celestial sign. They would have understood it as pointing to something extraordinary—a royal birth, according to their interpretation of celestial events.

Thus, this story in Matthew intertwines with the astrological themes of the time, bringing together cultural and spiritual elements, which later became central to the Christmas narrative.

The truth of the matter however, is that the real story is an astrological one. The Three Kings are the name of the three stars in Orion's Belt (a constellation), that in ancient times aligned with the bright star in the east (Sirius) to locate or point to a location on the horizon where the sun would rise on December 25th.

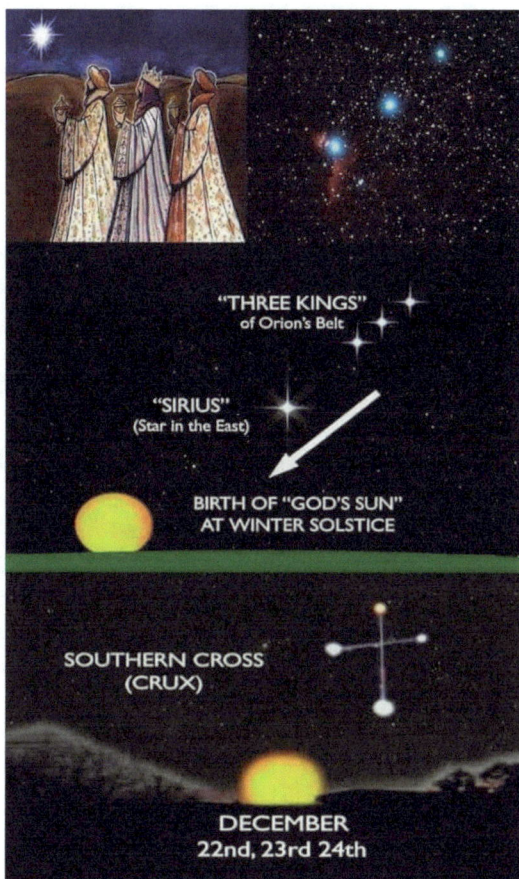

"THREE KINGS" of Orion's Belt

"SIRIUS" (Star in the East)

BIRTH OF "GOD'S SUN" AT WINTER SOLSTICE

SOUTHERN CROSS (CRUX)

DECEMBER 22nd, 23rd 24th

And thus it can be said that the three kings followed the bright star in the East to locate the birth of the sun (the risen savior), the light of the world, who saves us from darkness (as it does every morning).

This astrological phenomenon also happened near the Crux Constellation in ancient times. As mentioned earlier, the constellations have moved over the last few thousand years, so you'll need astronomy software to verify or see this for yourself.

In summary, the establishment of December 25th as Christmas was a multi-faceted decision shaped by theological symbolism, astrological observations, cultural adaptation, and political strategy.

This date's selection was instrumental in transforming Christmas into a focal point of Christian celebration, intertwining rich traditions from diverse origins into a unified holiday that continues to evolve today.

Christmas in the Medieval Period

In the medieval period, Christmas took on a rich tapestry of traditions that reflected the evolving landscape of Christianity mingling with enduring pagan customs.

This era was a fascinating blend (a melting pot) where the sacred and the festive intertwined, making the celebration truly unique. During this time, Christmas was gradually becoming more prominent in the Christian calendar, partly due to its strategic timing at a point when midwinter celebrations were widespread across Europe.

December 25th, established as the date for Christ's birth, wasn't just a random choice. It served as a symbolic counterpoint to solstice celebrations, echoing the themes of light overcoming darkness.

In medieval thought, this time of year symbolized a spiritual struggle, representing the triumph of the "true sun" over the barren, bleak months of winter. In many ways, it was the Church's savvy move to ensure that Christianity was not only spiritually satisfying but also culturally relevant.

Medieval Christmas was marked by grand feasts, from opulent banquets in the manors of the wealthy to hearty gatherings in humble homes.

Feast days could last for nearly two weeks, extending through the Twelve Days of Christmas, concluding on the Feast of Epiphany. For the peasantry, these celebrations were a welcome respite from the year's labors, filled with merriment, music, and dance.

The Lord of Misrule

Revelers embraced revelry with gusto, often blurring lines between sacred veneration and festive amusement. The Lord of Misrule, a common figure during the period, symbolized this role reversal and disorder, embodying the spirit of creating joy amidst a rigidly hierarchical world.

The "Lord of Misrule" was a figure in medieval and early modern European tradition, especially prominent in England, who presided over the Christmas festivities and revelry, typically during the Twelve Days of Christmas.

Appointed by a noble household, a village, or even the royal court, this character embodied the spirit of chaos and reversal of social order, taking on a mock authority and leading the festivities with merry-making, games, and mischief.

The Lord of Misrule's role often involved playfully subverting norms, creating a topsy-turvy "world turned upside down" atmosphere where servants might give orders to masters, and general antics were encouraged.

This reversal of hierarchy symbolized a temporary break from societal order, embodying the idea of a world in playful disarray before the return to routine with the end of the Christmas season.

Similar figures existed across Europe: in Scotland, the "Abbot of Unreason" took on a comparable role, and in France, the "Prince des Sots" (Prince of Fools) led similar revels.

The tradition faded by the 17th century, partly due to disapproval from the Puritans, who opposed such celebrations and sought to remove these carnival-like elements from Christmas.

Nativity Plays

Churches and chapels would echo with the sounds of the *Missa de Angelis* or nativity plays, which piqued the imaginations of medieval congregants. These plays often incorporated a good dose of humor and local color, revealing how seamlessly Christian narratives could be woven into the fabric of community storytelling.

Interspersed with high drama, these tales delivered biblical messages in a relatable way, showcasing medieval creativity and devotion.

Perhaps lesser-known, but equally enchanting, were the "Mystery Plays," popular during the later Middle Ages.

These dramas brought biblical stories to life thanks to the vivid portrayal by guild members who found not only spiritual but also communal connection through their performance. In medieval towns and cities, these productions became key events on the civic calendar, meshing sacred with spontaneous bursts of laughter and life.

At its core, Medieval Christmas was a time of community, deeply ingrained with the layers of cultural and religious evolution. It marked a pivotal chapter as Christmas matured, reflecting society's complex interweaving of tradition and belief—a vivid reminder of how the past continually reshapes what we understand about one of the world's most cherished holidays.

Mythological Syncretism: Parallels with Other Deities

In the Medieval Period, Christmas was more than just a celebration of Christ's birth; it was a tapestry woven with threads of various mythologies. The holiday's integration of different deities and traditions is a testament to the syncretic nature of medieval spirituality.

As Christian missionaries and conquerors spread through Europe, they encountered pagan practices deeply rooted in the cultures they aimed to convert, necessitating some degree of syncretism to pave the way for Christianity's acceptance.

This cultural blending wasn't a hasty process. In many cases, the absorption of pagan elements operated subtly, infusing long-held beliefs with Christian significance rather than eradicating them. A clear example of this syncretism is found in how certain deities were reinterpreted within the Christian framework.

Consider the enduring image of the sun god, prevalent in many European traditions. For cultures reliant on agriculture, the sun was revered as a vital life force, celebrated in festivals marking its journey across the sky. Over time, elements of these ancient solar celebrations mingled with the Christian narrative, lending Christmas a luminescent, broader significance that was more palatable to converts.

The Norse god Odin, with his long beard and mysterious, watchful nature, offers another striking parallel. Aspects of Odin were brought into the Christmas fold, influencing the legends surrounding Saint Nicholas and the later figure of Santa Claus.

In England, the figure of Father Christmas bore resemblances to pagan spirits of good cheer who blessed the winter season's feasting and merriment. These syncretic figures provided familiar bridges between the old beliefs and new Christian doctrines.

The fusion of mythologies during the medieval period was not merely a religious strategy but also a cultural necessity. It allowed disparate communities to maintain their unique identities while joining the burgeoning Christian world.

This blending of mythological elements in Christmas traditions has left an indelible mark on how we celebrate the holiday, illustrating how ancient customs and stories continue to resonate within modern festivities.

Impact of the Reformation on Christmas Celebrations

In the grand tapestry of Christmas, the Protestant Reformation stands out as a pivotal thread that shaped the festival in ways both profound and lasting.

The Reformation was a seismic shift in the religious landscape of Europe during the 16th century, stirred up more than just theological debate—it left its mark on cherished traditions, including Christmas.

Before the Reformation, Christmas celebrations across Europe were characterized by a medley of ecclesiastical observances and exuberant communal festivities. However, as Martin Luther and other reformers challenged the Catholic

Church's authority and practices, the very fabric of Christian holidays came under scrutiny. It wasn't just about doctrine; it was also about how one celebrated faith through such occasions as Christmas.

In areas where Protestantism took root, there was a notable shift in how Christmas was perceived and celebrated. Reformers often sought to strip away what they saw as remnants of paganism or Catholic tradition.

This included many Christmas customs that had evolved over centuries. In some regions, decorations, feasts, and the more boisterous elements of the holiday were viewed with suspicion or even outright disapproval. The focus, reformers argued, should return to the simplicity and piety of scriptural observance.

Yet, not all branches of Protestantism interpreted or implemented these changes the same way. For instance, while the English Puritans went so far as to ban Christmas during the mid-17th century, other groups, like the Lutherans, were more accommodating, advocating for a return to more Christ-centered festivities without abolishing the celebration altogether.

Banning Christmas?

Yes, the English Puritans, led by Oliver Cromwell and the Parliamentarians, famously banned Christmas celebrations in the mid-17th century.

During the English Civil War, the Puritans gained control over England and sought to reform the Church of England and remove practices they considered "popish" or indulgent. Christmas, with its feasting, revelry, and associations with pagan traditions, was viewed as excessive and un-Christian in their eyes.

In 1644, the Puritan-controlled Parliament declared Christmas a regular working day, and by 1647, they officially banned Christmas celebrations throughout England, along with other holidays they deemed frivolous.

This ban included prohibiting traditional feasts, decorations, and public gatherings, as well as closing shops and markets to curb celebratory activities. Instead, they promoted a day of fasting and reflection, aligning with their austere (severe or strict) values.

The ban on Christmas was highly unpopular, sparking riots and protests, especially among the working class, who saw it as an attack on their traditional customs. When the monarchy was restored in 1660 under King Charles II, the ban was lifted, and Christmas celebrations resumed.

This period of suppression, however, left a lasting impact on English attitudes toward Christmas, leading to a more subdued observance until the holiday was revived in the 19th century with Victorian reforms.

Despite the reforming zeal, the cultural deep roots of Christmas proved resilient. Practices that reformers attempted to suppress were often maintained in private or shifted until later holidays.

Over time, some of these traditions were re-incorporated into the broader celebration, albeit with a new Christian context. Thus, the Reformation did not extinguish Christmas festivities; rather, it countered excessive celebration and theological excess, which led to a reshaping that balanced contemplation with celebration.

Ultimately, the Reformation's impact on Christmas was as much a cultural negotiation as it was a religious reformation. It set into motion a spectrum of observances across Europe, each reflecting the nuances of local belief and historical development.

This diversity of celebration and belief helped shape Christmas into a holiday that, even today, mirrors the many ways

Christians have historically navigated the space between faith and festivity.

Chapter 6:
Influence of Roman Festivals

The Romans knew how to throw a party, and their festivals became legendary, even shaping our modern holidays. Among the most notable influences on Christmas are Saturnalia and Sol Invictus.

These Roman festivities were celebrated with great enthusiasm, marked by feasting, gift-giving, and merrymaking, serving as a template for later Christmas traditions. They introduced elements that were too joyful and too deeply ingrained in cultural practices to be left behind when Christianity began to dominate the Roman Empire.

Saturnalia, originally a festival in honor of Saturn, the god of agriculture and time, was celebrated in late December. During this time, social norms were upended; slaves were served by their masters, and a carefree atmosphere prevailed.

The practice of gift-giving during Saturnalia likely influenced the exchange of presents during Christmas, seamlessly being absorbed into Christian customs. This festival emphasized social equality, albeit temporarily, and communal joy, attributes that would become central to the spirit of Christmas.

Next on the roster was Sol Invictus, the "Unconquered Sun." Celebrated on December 25th, it marked the birthday of this sun god, who was seen as a patron of soldiers.

When Emperor Aurelian declared Sol Invictus an official deity, it cemented the day as a major celebration. As

Christianity spread, the Church adopted this date for Christ's birth.

It was a strategic move; synchronizing the birth of Jesus with the celebration of Sol Invictus allowed the Church to ease the transition for converts used to these December celebrations.

The fusion of Roman festivals with Christian rites wasn't simply about convenience. It was a cultural amalgamation, breathing new life into ancient customs under a Christian guise, enriching what would become an enduring and evolving holiday—Christmas.

Saturnalia and Sol Invictus in Christmas

As we delve into the festive heart of ancient Rome, two captivating celebrations emerge—Saturnalia and Sol Invictus.

These revelries echo through the ages, leaving a lasting imprint on the Christmas we know today. To grasp the influence of these Roman festivals on Christmas, let's take a stroll down the bustling streets of Rome at the height of winter festivities.

Saturnalia, a feast held in honor of Saturn, the god of harvest, kicks off around December 17th. What begins as a single day of celebration soon snowballs into a week of indulgence.

With a vibrant spirit of liberty, roles were reversed: slaves dined with their masters, business halted, and the rigid structure of Roman society loosened, if only temporarily. The atmosphere brimmed with laughter, merriment, and a generous dose of gift-giving—a custom that finds echo in our modern Christmas traditions.

Then, just as Saturnalia's fires began to dim, the spotlight shifted to Sol Invictus, the Unconquered Sun. Officially marked by the Emperor Aurelian in 274 AD, the celebration occurred on December 25th, just as the sun reached its nadir***** and promised its return.

Dedicated to the Syrian sun god, this holiday was a poignant reminder of life's resilience and renewal amid the cold expanse of winter. As Christianity spread through the Roman Empire, December 25th was seamlessly adopted, giving a familiar date to the nascent Christian festival.

These festivities, both raucous and reverent, offered Romans a profound sense of hope and belonging. As Christmas traditions evolved, the joyous anarchy of Saturnalia and the solemn symbolism of Sol Invictus found new expressions within a Christian framework. The shared themes of renewal and light persevered, knitting together the rich tapestry of Christmas that still warms our winter hearts.

Footnote:

- Nadir refers to the lowest point or most unsuccessful moment in a situation. It can describe a physical, metaphorical, or astronomical low. In astronomy, the nadir is the point in the sky directly beneath an observer, opposite the zenith (the highest point in the sky directly overhead). We discussed the sun's lowest point in Chapter One. In broader usage, the term often describes the lowest point of someone's fortunes, efforts, or an experience. For instance, "*The company's reputation reached its nadir after the scandal.*"

Incorporation of Roman Festivities into Christmas Celebrations

When we look at the tapestry of Christmas traditions, it becomes evident that Roman festivals played a significant role in shaping the holiday as we know it today.

The Romans, with their penchant for elaborate celebrations, particularly during the winter, set the stage for many customs that seamlessly transitioned into Christmas lore. Notably, the festivities of *Saturnalia* and the observance of *Sol Invictus* exerted a considerable influence on early Christmas celebrations.

Saturnalia, a raucous festival dedicated to Saturn, the god of agriculture and time, was marked by revelry, role reversals, and a general suspension of societal norms. This week-long celebration, typically held in mid-December, featured feasting, gift-giving, and the lighting of candles, elements that find echoes in modern Christmas traditions.

Many scholars argue that the practice of gift-giving during Christmas can be traced back to the exchanges made during Saturnalia, a time when Romans expressed goodwill amongst friends, family, and, often, their slaves.

Then there was *Sol Invictus*, the celebration of the "Unconquered Sun" on December 25th, which marked the renewal of light. This feast was linked to the sun god—a central figure in Roman pagan worship, symbolizing victory and the triumph of light over darkness.

It's no mere coincidence that the early Christian church chose this date for Christmas, strategically positioning the birth of Christ as a new light for the world, echoing the rebirth of the sun celebrated by Romans.

The synthesis of these Roman festivities into Christmas wasn't purely organic. In many ways, it was a calculated effort by early Christians to ease the transition from pagan practices to Christian worship.

By aligning Christmas with existing Roman festivals, the church effectively facilitated a cultural transition, offering familiar festivities while slowly imbuing them with Christian meaning. This strategic adaptation allowed Christmas to flourish amidst a tapestry of traditions, ultimately becoming remarkably inclusive and widespread.

As we unpack the culmination of these influences, it's clear that Christmas embodies a rich blend of ancient customs and Christian ideology. The Romans laid the groundwork with their vibrant festivals, crafting traditions that would endure the test of time.

Through this seamless incorporation, the essence of both Roman exuberance and spiritual rebirth contributes to the lively essence of Christmas, as it continues to evolve into a celebration appreciated across cultures and histories.

Chapter 7:
The Commercialization of Christmas

As we've journeyed through the rich tapestry of Christmas's evolution, we now explore a more modern transformation: its commercialization.

The holiday, once steeped in spiritual tradition and familial reverence, began to morph significantly as societies industrialized and capitalism took root. This shift wasn't just about the material but also how Christmas has been marketed and perceived over time.

In the late 19th and early 20th centuries, Christmas started to resemble what we know today, fueled by stronger economies and changing cultural attitudes. The rise of department stores brought with them the now-iconic Christmas window displays, turning city streets into festive wonderlands.

Retailers saw potential and seized upon the opportunity, transforming a religious and cultural observance into a bustling period of consumerism. These stores weren't just selling merchandise; they were selling an experience, a chance to partake in the magic of Christmas through spending.

Advertising became a powerful tool in Christmas's commercialization. With the advent of print media, radio, and later television, marketers crafted an image of Christmas that equated gift-giving with love and happiness.

Ad campaigns painted vivid pictures of familial warmth, often centered around a beautifully decorated tree. Coca-Cola famously reshaped Santa Claus's image, giving him the plump, jolly form we recognize today. This version of Santa became a symbol not just of Christmas spirit but of consumer indulgence.

However, it's not just about the gifts. The commercialization of Christmas blurred geographical lines, spreading the holiday's influence worldwide, sometimes at the expense of local traditions.

The global marketplace allowed Christmas symbols, like the Christmas tree and Santa Claus, to reach even the remotest corners, often overshadowing native customs. This aspect of globalization brought its own cultural shifts, leaving us pondering the holiday's true essence amidst the glitz and to-do lists.

In pondering these changes, we must ask: Has Christmas become a celebration of capitalism, or does the spirit of connection and generosity still hold sway?

While gifts and decorations take center stage, the underlying tensions between tradition and modernity continue to unfold, playing out each December in homes and businesses alike.

Market Expansion and Economic Impact of Christmas

The commercialization of Christmas was not an overnight phenomenon but a gradual evolution, shaped by expanding market dynamics that transformed the holiday from a sacred religious observance into a global economic powerhouse.

As the holiday grew in popularity, it became an essential period for retailers and service providers who capitalized on the season's festive spirit and generous consumer behavior.

In the mid-19th century, enterprising merchants recognized the season's economic potential. Department stores led the way, creating elaborate window displays and offering special holiday promotions to encourage seasonal spending.

This period marked the beginning of Christmas as not just a time for faith and family, but also an opportunity for consumer indulgence, reshaping both economic practices and cultural customs.

Today, the economic impact of Christmas extends far beyond retail gift sales, influencing a broad spectrum of industries. Total spending on holiday gifts, decor, events, and food reaches hundreds of billions annually.

The market for decorations alone, including trees, lights, ornaments, and outdoor displays, accounts for billions of dollars globally. The entertainment industry, too, sees a Christmas boom, with seasonal films, music, and themed events driving significant revenue. The food industry flourishes as well, as families and communities celebrate with festive feasts, specialty foods, and beverages that reflect the season's spirit.

Holiday travel and hospitality also benefit from the Christmas rush, with increased bookings for hotels, flights, and restaurants as people gather to celebrate together.

Additionally, shipping and logistics industries experience unprecedented demand as gifts, decorations, and holiday goods are transported around the world to meet seasonal expectations.

To reach consumers, advertising campaigns play a major role, evoking the holiday's themes of warmth, generosity, and family, further embedding Christmas as a time of abundance and connection.

The economic impact of Christmas is now a global phenomenon, from major retail chains to small businesses, all influenced by this period of heightened activity. What began as a set of religious observances has grown into a critical component of the annual financial cycle, as essential to economic planning as it is to cultural life.

The modern Christmas season embodies the blend of tradition, consumerism, and economic growth, evolving into an event as financially significant as it is culturally celebrated.

Holiday Spending

Here's a breakdown of estimated spending on various aspects of Christmas both in the United States and globally:

In the United States, total holiday spending is approximately $1 trillion in total holiday **Retail Sales** for November and December (National Retail Federation, NRF).

Money that Americans spend on **Gifts** is estimated to be around $650-$700 billion on holiday gifts each year. For decorations, we spend about $6 billion on Christmas decorations in the U.S., including trees, lights, wreaths, and other holiday decor.

Food and Beverages are estimated to be roughly $65 billion spent on holiday meals and drinks, as well as specialty foods and snacks for gatherings and celebrations.

The **Travel Industry** is estimated at over $20 billion spent on holiday-related travel in the U.S., including flights, accommodations, and road trips.

Holiday **Events and Entertainment** are estimated to be around $5 billion spent on entertainment, including tickets to seasonal events, movies, holiday shows, and theme parks.

For **Charitable Donations**, many Americans make donations during the holiday season, contributing around $30 billion annually.

Global Spending

For global holiday season spending, Total Holiday **Retail Sales** can reach around $1.5-$2 trillion, depending on various factors and economic conditions. International spending on holiday **Gifts** is estimated at approximately $1 trillion, with countries like the UK, Canada, Australia, and European nations having high per-capita gift spending.

Around $10-$15 billion is spent on holiday **Decorations** globally. Worldwide spending on Christmas **Food and Beverages** is estimated at $100 billion, with European countries also prioritizing festive meals and specialty foods.

Christmas **Travel** spending globally is approximately $50 billion, with major travel occurring in North America, Europe, and parts of Asia. Holiday-themed **Entertainment** (movies, events, theme parks) accounts for roughly $10 billion worldwide.

And lastly, charitable **Donations** around Christmas reach approximately $100 billion globally, with an increase in giving during the season across many cultures.

These figures vary year to year, but they highlight the economic influence of the Christmas season across different sectors and regions. The holiday remains a major driver of economic activity, reflecting its deep-rooted cultural significance worldwide.

Advertising Influence and Cultural Shifts in Christmas

As we segue into the bustling corridors of modern capitalism, it's clear that the kaleidoscope of Christmas has been dramatically reshaped by the insatiable whims of advertising.

The holiday, once steeped solely in spiritual and familial tradition, has been gently but persistently nudged into the realm of commercial spectacle. This metamorphosis owes much to the art (and some might argue, the science) of advertising.

From the latter half of the 19th century onward, businesses keen to expand their market reach have harnessed the imagery and sentiment of Christmas to conjure desires and drive sales.

In the early 20th century, advertisers began to craft seasonal campaigns that did more than just promote products. They shaped public perception and expectations of the holiday itself.

Perhaps the most iconic example of this is Coca-Cola's role in popularizing the jolly, red-suited image of Santa Claus.

While Santa's merry figure has historical roots, the Coke advertisements from the 1930s emblazoned him across the collective conscious, melding his figure with their signature branding. It was a masterstroke of advertising that blurred the lines between tradition and market interest, solidifying a cultural touchstone that persists to this day.

The post-war economic boom further amplified the commercial dimensions of Christmas. With newfound affluence, families were not only able to give gifts but were also encouraged to do so lavishly.

Advertisements played a crucial role in this new norm, featuring everything from toys to appliances as the *must-have* gifts of the season. Retailers capitalized on the emotive storytelling that these ads offered, tying products to the joy and warmth of holiday gatherings.

Television became a pivotal tool in transmitting these new Christmas archetypes. As people across the globe tuned in, they also tuned into a uniform vision of what Christmas should be—a perfectly wrapped confluence of family, generosity, and consumer delight.

Here lies a cultural shift: Christmas evolved from a religious observance entwined with local customs to a worldwide cultural phenomenon, largely standardized by the glossy sheen of ads.

Yet, while some may lament the commercialization of such a sacred time, others see it as an adaptive tradition, engaging in a dialogue with the times while still rooted in a spirit of giving and togetherness.

Advertising has not merely reflected cultural shifts; it has played a proactive role in catalyzing change. In our contemporary era, where digital marketing reigns, the holiday continues to adapt.

Social media platforms buzz with festive promotions, ready to dictate the next wave of consumer trends. This transformative power of advertising, while sometimes critiqued for diluting traditions, underscores an intricate interplay between market forces and cultural norms.

Through it, Christmas continues its journey of evolution—a testament to both the resilience and adaptability of seasonal celebrations in the face of ever-shifting societal landscapes.

Holiday Advertising Costs

In the U.S. and globally, holiday advertising represents a significant chunk of annual ad spending. Here are the approximate numbers for holiday advertising spending:

In the United States, Holiday Season **Advertising** is estimated to be around $20 billion spent on holiday advertising in the U.S. during the November-December period, targeting both Black Friday and Christmas shoppers.

Digital ads account for a large portion, with an estimated $7-10 billion dedicated to online channels, including social media, search engines, and video platforms. Television ads still remain popular for reaching holiday audiences, with about $5-7 billion spent on TV spots alone.

Print, Radio, and Outdoor Advertising are traditional media channels that collectively capture about $3 billion of the holiday advertising budget.

Worldwide Markets

As far as worldwide or global **Holiday Advertising** goes, holiday advertising spending reaches around $60-$70 billion across various regions.

Digital Spending dominates international holiday ad budgets, with about $30 billion spent on digital ads targeting holiday shoppers worldwide.

Global **Television Advertising** for the holiday season represents around $15 billion, with significant investment in regions like Europe, Asia, and Latin America.

In **Print, Radio, and Outdoor Advertising**, approximately $10 billion is spent across print, radio, and outdoor advertising on a global scale during the holiday season.

The U.S. leads in per-capita holiday ad spending, given the intense focus on holiday retail here, but when comparing total global spending, the combined worldwide ad spend does outpace the U.S. alone.

The U.S. holiday ad spend is substantial, reaching around $20 billion, and is one of the largest single-country ad budgets for the season. However, the total global holiday advertising spend, estimated at $60-$70 billion, is considerably higher when looking at all regions combined.

Evolution of Christmas Gift-Giving Traditions

In tracing the roots of Christmas gift-giving, you find yourself journeying through history, where the tradition sprouted from a web of cultural exchanges and transformations. What seems like a straightforward act today—the exchange of gifts—has experienced quite the metamorphosis over the centuries, driven significantly by commercialization.

Long before brightly wrapped presents were stashed under Christmas trees, the notion of exchanging gifts was tied to both spiritual and communal practices.

The Romans had their *Saturnalia*, during which gifts were exchanged in celebration of Saturn, the agricultural deity. These exchanges were modest by today's standards: candles, small figurines, and festive tokens, items meant to symbolize good luck and prosperity for the year ahead. Such practices created a foundation from which later holiday traditions could evolve.

The march of time brought with it the adaptation and transformation of these gift-giving rituals by early Christians.

During the Middle Ages, the tradition continued to evolve more into what we recognize today when in some places, the focus around gift-giving began to associate closely with the story of the Magi bringing gifts to the newborn Jesus. However, it wasn't until much later that the festive practice began to take on its modern commercial sheen.

The Victorian era marked a turning point. With the Industrial Revolution's machinery producing consumer goods en masse, merchants seized the opportunity to create a commercial boom around holiday celebrations.

Gift-giving began shifting from homemade and personal items to store-bought goods, spurred by burgeoning advertising campaigns that depicted gift-giving as an expression of love and status. Magazines and newspapers at the time started touting products as "must-have" items for the holiday season, sowing the seeds of modern consumerism.

Fast forward to the early 20th century, and mass media pushed this trend further. The portrayal of a jolly, red-suited Santa Claus by artists like Haddon Sundblom for Coca-Cola exemplified the burgeoning commercialization.

Suddenly, gifts weren't just a symbol of goodwill—they were increasingly tied to economic prosperity and personal expression.

As globalization expanded, so did the exchange of Christmas customs across borders. The American influence on Christmas gift-giving began to spread worldwide, blending with local traditions to create a myriad of unique cultural expressions.

While the underlying message of joy and generosity remains, the commercial aspect continues to dominate, as holiday sales become a critical economic driver for retailers globally.

The evolution of Christmas gift-giving traditions is a testament to the holiday's dynamic nature, reflecting changes in society's values and economic conditions. From its modest origins to its current commercial powerhouse status, this tradition underscores a complex interplay between culture, commerce, and the timeless human spirit of giving.

Globalization of Christmas Celebrations

As the twinkling lights of Christmas spread across the globe, the holiday becomes a canvas painted with diverse cultural brushstrokes.

What once was a winter solstice festival in Europe has morphed into a global phenomenon, bringing along an economic engine driven by the gears of globalization.

This international embrace of Christmas has transformed it from a primarily religious observance into a worldwide cultural event, knitted tightly into the fabric of global commercialism.

The rise of global trade and communication has been instrumental in this transformation. As businesses look beyond borders to tap into promising markets, the Christmas holiday acts as a key opening to these international doors.

Countries around the world have adopted and adapted Christmas traditions, often blending them with local customs to craft unique holiday expressions.

In Japan, for example, Christmas is **not** a national holiday, yet it is celebrated with enthusiasm, incorporating local flair with events and decorations that glitter with familiarity and novelty alike. A bucket of fried chicken on Christmas Eve (a tradition birthed from a successful marketing campaign) now stands as an emblem of a Japanese Christmas.

Global brands and their advertising prowess play a pivotal role in this cultural amalgamation, redefining traditional elements to suit local tastes while reinforcing a common, consumer-driven narrative.

The power of mass media spreads images of a jolly Santa operating in snow-dappled landscapes, pushing universal symbols of cheer and generosity. While for some, the globalization of Christmas is a moment of shared humanity, showcasing the universality of joy and generosity, it also raises questions about the holiday's true essence and the endurance of age-old traditions against a backdrop of commercial dominance.

The swap of local traditions for globally recognized symbols can sometimes eclipse indigenous practices. As television commercials and global franchises project a homogenized image of the holiday, there remains a delicate dance between maintaining local identity and embracing a standardized version of festive celebration.

The narrative thread of Christmas may be woven together by commercial interests, but underneath, a myriad of localized stories persists—a testament to the resilience of regional culture.

This globalization has, however, contributed substantially to the commercialization of Christmas. Gifts and consumer products flood markets worldwide, firing up economic activities each season.

From bustling Christmas markets in Germany to the lavish store windows on Fifth Avenue, the season signals a peak time for shopping, with industries tailoring their strategies to accommodate both traditional and newly adopted customer demands.

In essence, the globalization of Christmas celebrations reflects both the promises and challenges of our interconnected world. The holiday brings forth a shared platform for cultural exchange, inviting new interpretations while provoking significant reflection on what Christmas means beyond its commercial packaging.

Balancing these forces of change and tradition will define how future generations perceive and celebrate Christmas, ensuring it remains a holiday both richly global and deeply personal.

Chapter 8:
Modern Christmas Traditions

As the world spun through centuries, Christmas evolved, shedding layers like old coats and donning new ones stitched with threads of modernity and commerce.

Nowadays, Christmas is not merely a religious celebration; it embodies a mosaic of customs, often influenced by secular elements. These traditions, vibrant as a jolly snow globe scene, have captivated hearts and altered the festival's essence substantially.

One can't help but notice how commercialization has become the star on top of the contemporary Christmas tree. The once holy day now finds itself intertwined with aggressive marketing tactics.

Retailers, with their persuasive jingles and dazzling displays, invite consumers to embrace the spirit of giving, where giving often translates into buying. The impact is hard to ignore—the season seems as much about financial exchange as it is about familial warmth and spiritual reflection.

On the flip side, Christmas literature and media have played an undeniably pivotal role in shaping today's festive spirit. Classic tales like "*A Christmas Carol*" or modern retellings found in holiday movies paint narratives that blend tradition with contemporary values.

These stories encourage audiences to reflect on kindness, generosity, and joy, albeit through the lens of twenty-first-century storytelling techniques and technological advances.

Despite such universal themes, regional variations continue to flourish, adding rich tapestries to the global celebration. Each location adds its own distinct flavor—be it the spicy warmth of Mexican tamales or the elegance of Japanese KFC dinners.

Technology further diversifies these experiences, as virtual gatherings and digital greetings redefine connections in an interconnected world.

Of course, with these transformations come contemporary issues. Environmental concerns echo louder each year, challenging over-consumption and waste. This invites individuals to rethink and possibly revamp their traditions to be more sustainable.

Thus, as Christmas continues to express its dynamic nature, it reminds us that change—like tradition—is an inevitable, intricate dance. The dance keeps the spirit alive, weaving new meanings as it pirouettes through time.

Development of Contemporary Christmas Customs and Symbols

As Christmas has evolved through the ages, its customs and symbols have been shaped by a rich tapestry of cultural influences. The contemporary Christmas landscape we know today reflects how these elements have been molded by both personal experiences and broader social changes.

Often, it seems that these traditions carry a unique ability to strike a chord that resonates, not just because they're steeped in history, but because they continually adapt to each new generation.

Consider the Christmas tree, for instance. What was once a symbol reserved for the aristocracy in 19th-century Europe has now become a centerpiece in homes across the globe, regardless of creed.

The evergreen tree, cherished for its steadfastness through winter, has long symbolized resilience and hope. Today's Christmas trees might shimmer with electric lights and an array of ornaments; these adornments represent both a nod to the past and a reflection of our relentless appetite for progress and innovation.

This commercial progression arguably reached a pinnacle with the transformation of Saint Nicholas into the beloved figure of Santa Claus.

Initially rooted in Sinterklaas stories from the Netherlands, Santa Claus was further popularized through 19th-century literature, fueled by the astonishing illustrations of magazines and the poetic musings of writers. It wasn't long before Santa Claus emerged as a charismatic icon, intertwining seamlessly with his role in commerce and media.

Another essential contemporary symbol is the holiday feast, echoing the communal gatherings of old solstice celebrations. While the core idea of sharing meals remains a staple, each region adds its own flavor, a secret recipe brought over by immigrants or a creative reinterpretation of ancient tastes. This culinary melting pot reflects the diversity inherent in modern Christmas traditions.

The exchange of gifts further exemplifies how customs persist and change. Initially tied to religious and spiritual meanings, the act has been transformed by commercial forces into a dazzling display of affection and consumerism. Yet beneath this commercial veneer, the ritual maintains its deeper roots in kindness and connection, a testament to its enduring allure.

As society continues to change, these traditions will inevitably evolve further. While some worry that the essence of Christmas may be lost amidst flashy new innovations, others embrace the holiday's capacity to absorb new influences while retaining its core message of joy, solidarity, and renewal.

Indeed, this dynamic interplay is a hallmark of Christmas's enduring magic, one that continues to captivate hearts and homes worldwide.

The Impact of Commercialization on Modern Christmas Celebrations

When modern-day Christmas rolls around, it's almost impossible to ignore the glitz and glamor that seem to surround the holiday.

With decorated store windows, elaborate ad campaigns, and an incessant push to buy the perfect gift, commercialization has undeniably reshaped how Christmas is celebrated today. This transformation didn't happen overnight. Instead, it crept in gradually, weaving itself into the very fabric of the holiday.

For many, the holiday season now kicks off not with whispers of snow or the aroma of freshly baked gingerbread but with Black Friday deals and Cyber Monday madness.

Retailers put on a dazzling display, each trying to outdo the other, hoping to capture the lion's share of the festive spending spree. What started as a religious and family-centered affair has, in many ways, become a commercial marathon.

But what does this mean for the essence of Christmas?

The birth of Christ seems increasingly distant against the backdrop of overindulgence and consumerism. Christmas has become less about heartfelt exchanges and more about ticking items off a list, driven by clever marketing and a fear of missing out.

The jolly image of Santa Claus, originally based on the charitable Saint Nicholas, has played its part too. Today, Santa is often viewed more like the ambassador of big brands, rather than the patron of giving and kindness.

Embedded within these changes, however, lies an intriguing dance between innovation and tradition. On one hand, commercialization has democratized Christmas, allowing everyone to partake in its festivities regardless of their diverse backgrounds.

On the other hand, it raises questions about the values we wish to pass on to future generations. Are we inadvertently teaching them to equate love with material wealth?

At the same time, commercialization has been a double-edged sword. It's fostered a sense of collective cheer and excitement, funneled funds into local economies, and generated seasonal jobs.

The holiday season is a critical economic driver, breathing life into sectors that might otherwise struggle. Yet, it also places a colossal strain on individuals, urging them to spend beyond their means and potentially casting a shadow on the true spirit of giving.

The challenge, then, is striking a balance. How do we maintain the joyous and inclusive nature of modern Christmas without losing its spiritual and cultural underpinnings?

It's a question worth pondering as we continue to celebrate this cherished holiday in both traditional and new ways.

Influence of Christmas Literature and Media

Christmas, as we experience it today, owes much to the rich tapestry of literature and media that has evolved alongside the holiday. These cultural artifacts have not just mirrored Christmas traditions but have also actively shaped them, embedding ideas, images, and emotions into the collective consciousness.

It all started in the 19th century with Charles Dickens' "*A Christmas Carol.*" This tale didn't merely depict a Victorian celebration; it reshaped Christmas into a season of generosity and goodwill.

Dickens painted a picture of England where even the coldest hearts could find warmth in the glow of familial love and charity. Scrooge's journey from miser to benefactor reinforced the notion that Christmas was a time for compassion and personal transformation.

Moving into the modern era, literature has continued to redefine the holiday. From Dr. Seuss's *"How the Grinch Stole Christmas!"* to more recent works, stories of redemption, magic, and joy have continuously expanded and enriched our understanding of Christmas. Each narrative, whether through descriptions of mystical snowfalls or transformed, joyous bustling cities, adds another layer to the fabric of the holiday spirit.

Television and film have further amplified these themes, becoming central to how we view and celebrate Christmas. Classic films like *"It's a Wonderful Life"* and *"Miracle on 34th Street"* have become traditional viewing, embedding the season's morals and messages deep in our annual festivities.

These media portrayals are not passive; they actively participate in creating shared holidays if stories can bend reality. Over the years, contemporary holiday specials and movies have broadened the imagination, offering diverse ways to connect with the season. They continue to play a pivotal role in shaping perceptions, showcasing a Christmas that is equal parts nostalgic and reflective.

As technology progresses, new forms of media like streaming services have revolutionized how we engage with these stories, making them more accessible and varied than ever. The continuous narrative evolution keeps Christmas alive, ensuring its relevance across generations and cultures.

Thus, the influence of Christmas literature and media is profound, crafting not just a time of year but the very ethos of how it is celebrated. By presenting ideas that both honor tradition and invite new interpretations, literature and media do not merely observe what Christmas is—they help define what it means to us today.

Regional Variations in Christmas Celebrations

Even though the core of Christmas (celebrating joy, togetherness, and kindness) remains constant, the ways people around the world mark this holiday are as diverse as the regions themselves.

Each area molds Christmas traditions through its own cultural lens, offering a kaleidoscope of celebrations that reflect both local customs and global influences.

In **Europe**, for instance, there's a rich tapestry of traditions that make Christmas more than just a day on the calendar. In **Germany**, the Advent season is a major affair, marked by the daily excitement of opening Advent calendars and visiting bustling Christmas markets.

Meanwhile, **Italy** is known for its grand feasts, featuring dishes unique to each region, with seafood taking center stage in coastal areas. The **UK** has its own time-honored practices, with families gathering around the table for a Christmas dinner of roast turkey followed by the flamboyant lighting of the Christmas pudding.

Head down under to **Australia**, and Christmas takes on a summer vibe, where barbecues replace roast dinners, and beaches become the favorite gathering spots. It's a land where the heat dictates the festivity style, yet the same spirit of hospitality and merry-making endures.

Across the Atlantic, in the Americas, traditions vary widely too. In **Mexico**, the nine-day festival of Las Posadas re-enacts

Mary and Joseph's search for a place to stay, culminating in lively parties with piñatas for the children.

Over in **Brazil**, the Portuguese influence weaves through Christmas with the festive consoada meal and Missa do Galo (Midnight Mass), creating a blend of European customs and tropical flair.

The Nordic countries offer a magical blend of ancient pagan rituals and Christian celebrations. **Sweden's** Sankta Lucia Day, held on December 13th, is celebrated with candle-lit processions and is the harbinger of the festive season. In **Norway**, the Julenisse, a traditional gnome, brings joy to children, echoing the Santa Claus saga with a local twist.

Asia adds its unique flavors to Christmas, with traditions that adapt to local religions and practices. In **Japan**, Christmas has morphed into an occasion more focused on spreading happiness, often celebrated with KFC dinners (a quirky yet well-loved tradition) and romantic outings.

Though a minority, the Christian communities in countries like **India** and the **Philippines** celebrate with vibrant and colorful traditions, from midnight masses to star-shaped lanterns lighting up the night.

The essence of Christmas, although wrapped in various cultural fabrics, continues to be a celebration of goodwill and unity. These regional variations reflect a world that's rich in traditions, one where Christmas brings out the local flavor while highlighting shared human experiences.

Influence of Technology on Christmas

Over the years, technology has profoundly reshaped the way we celebrate Christmas, creating new traditions and adding layers of complexity to existing ones. As digital innovations permeate different regions of the world, they've injected a blend of uniformity and uniqueness into Christmas customs.

In some regions, the mode of celebration has gone from intimately local to dazzlingly global, thanks in large part to technology. Video calls have replaced traditional family gatherings for those separated by vast distances, allowing for a sense of togetherness despite being thousands of miles apart.

Live streaming of church services has enabled participation in religious ceremonies from the comfort of one's home, altering the traditional communal experience yet making it accessible for those who might otherwise miss out. In many ways, technology has made Christmas more inclusive, granting access to festivities that know no geographical limits.

Beyond facilitating connections, technology has also transformed the way people experience Christmas through regional variations. In urban centers, elaborate light displays synchronized with music can create a mesmerizing spectacle.

These high-tech shows have become a staple in some areas, attracting both locals and tourists who flock to witness the marriage of art and technology. In contrast, rural regions might still retain a more traditional approach to Christmas lighting, relying on simpler, handcrafted decorations that tell stories of heritage and cultural roots.

The rise of e-commerce has also injected a dynamic shift into holiday traditions around the world. Online shopping has streamlined the gift-giving process, affecting how people interact with the concept of giving itself.

In many places, storefront shopping retains its charm, but the convenience of app-based browsing and delivery often takes the spotlight, redefining what presents mean in various cultural contexts.

Meanwhile, social media plays a critical role in shaping Christmas traditions by providing a platform for both sharing and discovering new ideas. From the posting of festive family photos to the sharing of holiday recipes, individuals around the globe customize their celebrations by borrowing and blending diverse influences. This creates a tapestry of regional variations, each enriched by the interplay between technology and tradition.

Thus, technology serves as both a bridge and a catalyst in the evolving narrative of Christmas. As it nudges ancient customs toward modernity, it also fosters regional distinctiveness, ensuring that Christmas remains a richly varied celebration worldwide.

Environmental Concerns Related to Christmas Traditions

As we dive into the intricacies of modern Christmas traditions, it's impossible to overlook the environmental footprint that comes with the festivities. This awareness isn't just confined to one region; it's a global issue that casts a shadow over yuletide cheer.

Traditions that seem universal, like the iconic Christmas tree, have different impacts depending on where you are.

In regions where fir trees are abundant, the cutting and replanting cycle is a part of the ecological norm, yet the carbon footprint of transporting these trees across countries can't be ignored.

In urban areas, synthetic trees are popular as a more sustainable option, but they come with their own issues involving non-biodegradable materials and production emissions.

The lighting that's often seen as part and parcel of the Christmas spirit varies in environmental impact, too. In regions where electricity is predominantly generated from renewable sources, the twinkling lights may not be a burden on the environment.

However, in areas relying on fossil fuels, the charm of illuminated displays comes at a more significant environmental cost. Many communities are now opting for energy-efficient LED lights or reducing the hours they leave displays on.

Holiday feasts also paint a complex picture of regional environmental impact. While seasonal and locally sourced foods might dominate the menu in some areas, global supply chains ensure that exotic items appear on tables elsewhere, accompanied by a hefty carbon footprint.

The waste generated from packaging, especially in regions with robust gift-giving traditions, further complicates the situation. Many are turning to sustainable practices like reusable wrapping or digital gifting to mitigate this issue.

In summary, while Christmas celebrations have evolved and adapted to the cultural and regional nuances they encompass, the environmental implications demand attention.

Recognizing the disparity in ecological impacts across different regions can guide more sustainable choices, ensuring that the warmth of Christmas traditions doesn't come at the expense of the planet's health.

Contemporary Issues in Christmas Celebrations

In today's world, the manner in which Christmas is celebrated can vary widely depending on cultural, social, and economic factors. These variations bring with them a host of contemporary challenges and discussions that both enrich and complicate the season's festivities.

One of the prominent issues is the tension between secular and religious observances. In some regions, Christmas has taken on a predominantly secular tone, becoming more about universal symbols like Santa Claus and seasonal decorations, while in others, the focus remains deeply rooted in its religious origins.

This divergence often leads to debates about the 'true' meaning of Christmas, with some fearing the loss of spiritual significance amid growing commercialization.

Technological advancements have also shaped how Christmas is celebrated across the globe. The rise of digital communication allows families to connect across distances, yet it also introduces concerns about maintaining the warmth of personal interactions.

Online shopping has transformed gift-giving, making it more convenient but also contributing to environmental and economic concerns regarding overconsumption and waste.

Furthermore, environmental issues have become increasingly prominent in discussions about Christmas. The traditional practices, like using real Christmas trees or excessive lighting, are being reconsidered in light of modern environmental awareness. A push towards sustainable practices is gaining momentum, with an emphasis on eco-friendly decorations and mindful consumption.

Ultimately, the choice of how to celebrate Christmas is deeply personal and influenced by regional and cultural backgrounds.

These contemporary issues highlight the evolving nature of Christmas and the ongoing dialogue between preserving cherished traditions and adapting to present-day realities. It's this very interplay that keeps the holiday dynamic, allowing it to be both a reflection of past customs and a canvas for new interpretations.

Conclusion

In exploring the historical and cultural evolution of Christmas, we've traversed a path filled with fascinating intersections between pagan traditions and Christian interpretations.

From the ancient solstice celebrations to the cherished customs we observe today, this journey unveils the complex tapestry woven over centuries. Each chapter of this book has sought to highlight how Christmas, as we know it, stands on the shoulders of countless cultural exchanges and adaptations.

The roots of Christmas are deeply anchored in pre-Christian traditions. Early societies embraced the winter solstice, celebrating themes of death and rebirth with vibrant festivals, which influenced the timing and meaning of Christmas.

As we moved into the realm of pagan origins, we uncovered how ancient civilizations like the Sumerians, Akkadians, and Babylonians contributed rituals that echo through modern customs, such as the yule log and the reverence for solar deities.

The adaptation of these pagan traditions into early Christian practices marked a pivotal shift, driven by both religious and political motivations. Leaders like Constantine and Theodosius played crucial roles in shaping a festival that could unify an empire under the new Christian ethos, integrating syncretism and local customs along the way.

This transformation isn't just a historical footnote; it demonstrates the pragmatic flexibility of cultural traditions in response to changing societal contexts.

Saint Nicholas's mythic journey from a charitable bishop to the jolly figure of Santa Claus underscores the evolving nature of Christmas. His transformation reflects societal values and ideals at different times, embodying a spirit of generosity that transcends religious boundaries.

In parallel, the decision to establish December 25th as the day of celebration signifies the early church's strategic appropriation of existing festivals like Saturnalia, subtly aligning Christian doctrine with ingrained Roman customs.

The modern incarnation of Christmas bears witness to the powerful forces of commercialization and globalization. Economic imperatives have reshaped how we celebrate, influencing everything from gift-giving to the global reach of Christmas imagery.

Despite these shifts, the enduring cultural significance of Christmas remains resilient. It continues to foster a sense of community, reflection, and joy, while being a mirror of contemporary societal values and challenges, such as environmental concerns.

In reflecting on how Christmas has evolved over centuries, we're reminded that it's not merely a religious or secular holiday—it's a living tradition, a dynamic interweaving of the past and present.

Understanding this evolution deepens our appreciation of Christmas's multifaceted essence. As we celebrate, we engage in a rich dialogue between ancient symbols and contemporary practices, ensuring that this beloved holiday continues to evolve, resonate, and illuminate our shared human experience.

Summary of Key Points on Christmas Evolution

The journey of Christmas from its ancient roots to its current form is a tale of transformation and adaptation. We see the integration of pre-Christian traditions like the winter solstice's celebration of the sun's rebirth playing a significant role in shaping what we now know as Christmas.

These early influences provided a framework that Christianity later adopted and adapted, reshaping the spiritual narrative to fit the birth of Christ within these longstanding traditions.

Significant was the role of figures like Constantine, whose political maneuvers helped cement the blending of pagan and Christian practices. The establishment of December 25th as the date for Christmas showcases how strategic decisions interwove religious symbolism with pre-existing festivals like Saturnalia and Sol Invictus, further solidifying the holiday's place within the Christian context.

The transformation of Saint Nicholas into the modern Santa Claus is another fascinating layer of this evolution, illustrating the holiday's cultural fluidity. Similarly, the commercialization of Christmas highlights a shift from purely religious festivities to a global phenomenon marked by economic and social dynamics.

Today, Christmas wears many hats: sacred celebration, family tradition, and commercial enterprise, each adding new dimensions to its ongoing story.

Thus, the evolution of Christmas is a lens through which we can see the intersection of ancient customs and modern innovations, revealing a holiday continually reborn, much like the sun it originally celebrated.

Reflection on the Historical and Cultural Significance of Christmas

Christmas, a holiday now synonymous with joy, gift-giving, and family gatherings, has a rich tapestry woven through centuries of diverse cultural practices and religious beliefs.

Its evolution from pagan roots to a distinctly Christian celebration illustrates a fascinating journey of adaptation and transformation. At its core, Christmas embodies a unique confluence of traditions that have been shaped by historical events and cultural interchanges.

Throughout history, the time of year now celebrated as Christmas has held deep significance across various early cultures. The winter solstice marked a pivotal point, symbolizing the death and rebirth of the sun, a theme central to many ancient celebrations.

As these traditions made their way into the Christian narrative, they were adapted to fit the emerging religious framework, leading to a symbiotic relationship between pagan customs and Christian faith.

The significance of Christmas also lies in its ability to act as a mirror reflecting societal changes over the centuries.

From its early days as a minor celebration within Christianity to its establishment as a major holiday under rulers like Constantine and Theodosius, Christmas adapted to political and social landscapes. The intertwining of Roman festivals such as Saturnalia and Sol Invictus brought forth customs that continue to influence modern celebrations.

Moreover, Christmas's cultural significance has been bolstered by the figure of Saint Nicholas, whose transformation into the modern Santa Claus introduced elements of folklore and myth into the holiday. This evolution highlights how Christmas has been shaped by stories that transcend generations, each layer adding depth and character to the overall narrative.

In more recent centuries, the commercialization of Christmas has contributed to its widespread appeal and global celebration. While this shift has sparked debates over the holiday's true meaning, it has also underscored its role as a cultural touchstone that adapts to contemporary times. This ability to evolve while retaining core elements of joy, generosity, and togetherness underscores the enduring nature of Christmas.

Ultimately, the historical and cultural significance of Christmas is found in its malleability and resilience. It is a testament to the intricate interplay of diverse traditions, each leaving an indelible mark on the holiday as we know it today.

Christmas is not merely a celebration of religious significance; it is a vibrant kaleidoscope of historic legacy and cultural fusion, resonating with people across the globe in myriad ways.

About the Author

Robert Enochs is a self-educated researcher, author, and thinker with a deep-rooted passion for uncovering the hidden narratives that shape our history, society, and traditions.

Through extensive study and a relentless curiosity, he has cultivated a unique perspective on the intricate intersections of history, politics, and culture. Robert's work invites readers to question popular narratives and delve beneath the surface, encouraging a thoughtful examination of long-held beliefs.

This book, *The Origins and Evolution of Christmas: From Pagan Traditions to Modern Celebrations*, is the second installment in the *Mysteries of Tradition* series. In this journey through history and tradition, Robert takes readers into the fascinating transformation of Christmas, uncovering the layers of influence and ritual that have come to define the holiday.

For those interested in further exploration, the first book in the series, *The Origins and Evolution of Halloween*, offers an equally intriguing look into the ancient roots of another iconic celebration.

If you've enjoyed *The Origins and Evolution of Christmas*, please consider leaving a positive review on Amazon. Your feedback not only helps other readers discover this book but also supports the ongoing exploration of these intriguing subjects.

Robert appreciates your engagement and invites you to continue the journey through the *Mysteries of Tradition* series as we seek to understand the world beyond the ordinary.

Made in United States
Cleveland, OH
07 December 2024